Praise for *Copper Yearning*

"Kimberly Blaeser's books have always been necessary reading, but *Copper Yearning* takes things to an entirely different level. The poems in this spectacular collection demonstrate a heightened sense of political awareness and poetic experimentation. As a reader and as a citizen I was both challenged and rewarded. Moving from local acts of resistance like Standing Rock to global concerns like Indigenous land rights, Blaeser's poems feel like they are both timely and timeless. Best of all, her poems reflect a commitment to craft commensurate with the poems' thematic ambitions. This is a collection to read and reread for a lifetime."

—Dean Rader, author of *Self-Portrait as Wikipedia Entry*

"*Copper Yearning* is a marvelous kaleidoscope—a poetics that flows, as do liquid and silvers, from the elemental to the oracular 'Dreams of Water Bodies.' I love the musicality of Blaeser's lines, the sense of some invisible motion that pulses from line to line, poem to poem, a motion that is beyond time but manifests here in dynamic rhythm and form. These are poems of vivid alchemy that praise all forms of life: cartographic, geologic, animate, poetic. Blaeser travels through these forms with fervor and dexterity; each poem is a journey through immensity with its detail of this 'small magic we call earth' in all of its peculiar beauty."

—Jennifer Foerster, author of *Bright Raft in the Afterweather*

Books by Kimberly Blaeser

Poetry

Copper Yearning
(Holy Cow! Press), 2019

Apprenticed to Justice
(Salt Publishing), 2007

Absentee Indians and Other Poems
(Michigan State University Press), 2002

Trailing You (Greenfield Review Press), 1994

Editor

Traces in Blood, Bone, and Stone: Contemporary Ojibwe Poetry
(Loonfeather Press), 2006

Stories Migrating Home
(Loonfeather Press), 1999

Literary Studies

Gerald Vizenor: Writing in the Oral Tradition
(University of Oklahoma Press), 1996

COPPER YEARNING

Poems by Kimberly Blaeser

Holy Cow! Press
Duluth, Minnesota
2019

Author photograph by John Fisher.
Cover photograph, "Where Amber Light Spills," by Kimberly Blaeser.
Section 1, Picto-poem color plate, "Dreams of Water Bodies," by Kimberly Blaeser.
Book and cover design by Anton Khodakovsky.

Printed and bound in the United States.
First printing, Fall, 2019

ISBN 978-1513645612

10 9 8 7 6 5 4 3 2 1

Holy Cow! Press projects are funded in part by grant awards from the Ben and Jeanne Overman Charitable Trust, the Elmer L. and Eleanor J. Andersen Foundation, the Lenfestey Family Foundation, and by gifts from generous individual donors.

Holy Cow! Press books are distributed to the trade by Consortium Book Sales & Distribution, c/o Ingram Publisher Services, Inc., 210 American Drive, Jackson, TN 38301

For inquiries, please write to: HOLY COW! PRESS,
Post Office Box 3170, Mount Royal Station, Duluth, MN 55803
Visit *www.holycowpress.org*

For the ancestral lands

that birthed these yearnings.

For the Water Protectors—*ogichidaakweg*

who walk for health of *nibi*.

*   *   *

For Robert and Len—

companions and guides on the journey.

CONTENTS

ACKNOWLEDGMENTS

This gathering of poetry also represents a gathering of the kindnesses extended to me over the last decade while the work for this volume was being done. Poetry, like any other work we do, comes into being not only through the specific tasks like writing, research, and editing immediately involved in its creation, but rather evolves from a complex chain of interactions. The acknowledged buttresses of this collection include the inspiration of and collaboration with other writers, artists, educators, and activists; the opportunity to enter and dissolve into natural spaces for extended periods of time; the support and care I received in basic things from travel to materials collection to funding; the opportunities for performance and publishing; and the bracing humor and validation from my family and friends. For these and all other kinds of assistance and support, I offer deep appreciation.

Thanks in particular to the following books and journals and their gracious editors for publishing poems or earlier versions of poems that now appear in this volume.

Undocumented: Great Lakes Poets Laureate on Social Justice, Native Voices: Honoring Indigenous Poetry from North America, Thinking Continental: Writing the Planet One Place at a Time, Poetry of Presence: An Anthology of Mindfulness Poems, The World is One Place: Native American Poets Visit the Middle East, Sing: Poetry from the Indigenous Americas, Louis Owens: Writing Land and Legacy, Audelà du chagrin (Beyond Sorrow), We Contain Multitudes, Medvefelhő a város felett: Észak-amerikai indián költők antológiája, The Heath Anthology of American Literature, Amethyst and Agate: Poems of Lake Superior, The Sacred in Contemporary Haiku, Echolocations: Poets Map Madison, Turn Up the Volume: Poems about the States of Wisconsin, Ghost Fishing: An Eco-Justice Poetry Anthology.

Hayden's Ferry Review, Diálogo Magazine, Denver Quarterly, The Vassar Review, About Place Journal, Kenyon Review, New Letters, Levure littéraire, Literary Hub, Sentence: A Journal of Prose Poetics, Common-Place: The Journal of Early American Life, World Literature Today, Brain Mill Press, Yukhika-látuse: She Tells Stories, cream city review, Verse Wisconsin, Yahara Prairie Lights, The Leopold Outlook, The Municipality, Poets Respond to Madison, Mujeres Talk, Wisconsin Poets'

Calendar, Hybrid: Transported by Word and Image, Imagine Our Parks with Poems, Faith ND, Milwaukee Journal Sentinel, Native Literature: Generations, Yellow Medicine Review, Poetry Speaks, Future Earth, Pembroke Magazine.

Gratitude as well to Gaylord Shanilec, Wendy Vardaman. Daniel Goscha, and Debra Jircik for work on design, paper making, and letter press printing of stunning broadsides of my poetry.

Much appreciation to Jim Perlman and Holy Cow! Press—for the generous support of my work through this publication, but more importantly, for decades of respectful engagement with Native cultures and our book arts.

Chimiigwetch to Margaret Noodin for friendship, collaborations, language lessons, and her thoughtful translations of my poetry into *Anishinaabemowin*.

My appointment as Wisconsin Poet Laureate for 2015-2016 delightfully enhanced my experience as a "working poet." For this honor and the accompanying blessings of the post, I offer sincere thanks to the Wisconsin Poet Laureate Commission and the members of the commission with whom it has been my pleasure to work: Chuck Stebleton, Bill Stobbs, Ronnie Hess, Soham Patel, Ching-In Chen, Nick Demske, Max Garland, Richard Swanson, Kevin Miller, Carol Cohen, Sheri Castelnuova, Cathy Cofell, Brent Goodman, Angie Trudell Vasquez, Abayomi Animashaun, Karen Ann Hoffman, and Mark Zimmerman. Thank you to the University of Wisconsin-Milwaukee and, in particular, Chancellor Mark Mone and former Associate Dean for the College of Arts and Letters, Dave Clark, for their support of my work as Wisconsin Poet Laureate. My gratitude to all who assisted in my launch of the Poetry Recitation Map (*http://www.wisconsinpoetlaureate.org/poetry-in-wisconsin*) during my tenure. Applause and appreciation to all intrepid performers who have taken part in poetry-by-heart events or sent in videos. Keep them coming!

I am indebted as well to the following organizations with which I am associated for the invaluable work they do: Institute of American Indian Arts, Aldo Leopold Foundation, and the Wisconsin Academy of Sciences, Arts, & Letters. Gratitude to all with whom I have worked in those organizations, but especially to Jennifer Foerster, Jamie Figueroa, Jon Davis, Santee Frazier, Buddy Huffacker, Jennifer Kobylecky, Jane Elder, and Jason Smith.

I thank the Center for 21st Century Studies, the Wisconsin Arts Board, the Wisconsin Humanities Commission, the Electa Quinney Institute, The Academy of American Poets, Woodland Pattern Book Center, *To the Best of Our Knowledge*, Write On Door County, MMOC (Madison Museum of Contemporary Art), Wisconsin Fellowship of Poets, Cirenaica, *Wisconsin Life*, Chanzen

Museum, Shake Rag Alley, Oberholtzer Foundation, Center for the Book, UWM Field Station, Oak Lake Writers, Galena Center for the Arts, Jones Gallery, Union Art Gallery, Lorine Niedecker Festival, Milwaukee Native American Literary Cooperative, Gaylord Nelson Institute, *Wisconsin Writes*, and Eat Local, Read Local for various kinds of patronage including fellowships, grants, poetry features, exhibits, and residencies.

The list of those who have nourished me on this poetic journey include graduate students and workshop participants (Toby Wray, Shanae Aurora Martinez, Siwar Masannat, Peter Burzynski, Manny Loley, Rowena Alegria, Alessandra Simmons Rolffs, Franklin Cline, Kenzie Allen, Loretta Mccormick, Elisa Karbin, and many more), AIS and IAIA colleagues, editors, and the tireless promoters of poetry performance. I send blessings to each of you and to the writers from Rumi to Momaday whose words will ever inhabit me. I offer particular gratitude to fellow Crow Commons members Molly McGlennen, Jane Halliday, Gordon Henry, and Jesse Peters. The spirit and memory of Word Warriors Amy DeJarlais, Michael Roberts, and Lupe Solis also abide in my work. I remember here Susan Brill de Ramirez a brilliant scholar who generously turned her eye on my work. The members of Pros and Cons from Racine Correctional Institution remind me how poetry truly sustains us in any circumstance. Indeed, I would need another book to name all those who have graciously shared their gifts over the years, but I would be remiss if I did not offer a special shout out to Anne Kingsbury in her retirement; to Jen Benka, Denise Sweet, Sara Busse, Dean Rader, Joy Harjo, Fabu, Janet McAdams, Allison Hedge Coke, Linda Hogan, and Natalie Diaz, poets extraordinaire; and to Theresa Delgadillo, Laura Tohé, Luci Tapahonso, Chris LaLonde, John Purdy, Michael Wilson, Chris Fink, Denise Lajimodiere, and Cathy Waegner for sharing the many registers of friendship.

My final stanza of gratitude goes to my family who participate every day in the most basic and essential tasks of world making. When you feed me candid political conversations or old stories, venison sausage or dreamy BWCA paddles, you feed me poetry. Miigwech especially to Amber, Gavin, and Len; Robert, Lenor, Jason, Josh, Tami, and Gail.

PROEM

Wellspring: Words from Water

A White Earth childhood water rich and money poor.
Vaporous being transformed in cycles—
the alluvial stories pulled from Minnesota lakes
harvested like white fish, like *manoomin,*
like old prophecies of seed growing on water.
Legends of Anishinaabeg spirit beings:
cloud bearer Thunderbird who brings us rain,
winter windigo like Ice Woman, or *Mishibizhii*
who roars with spit and hiss of rapids—
great underwater panther, you copper us
to these tributaries of balance. Rills. A cosmology
of *nibi.* We believe our bodies thirst. Our earth.
One element. *Aniibiishaaboo.* Tea brown
wealth. Like maple sap. Amber. The liquid eye of moon.
Now she turns tide, and each wedded being gyrates
to the sound, its river body curving.
We, women of ageless waters, endure;
like each flower drinks from night,
holds dew. Our bodies a libretto,
saturated, an aquifer—we speak words
from ancient water.

I.

GEOGRAPHIES OF LONGING

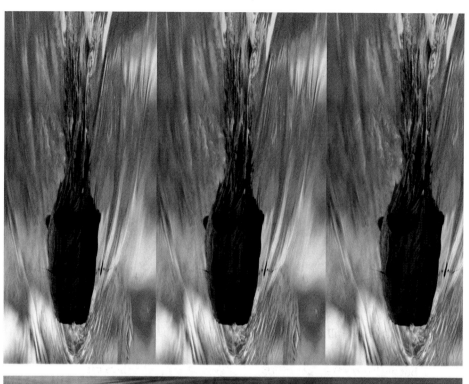

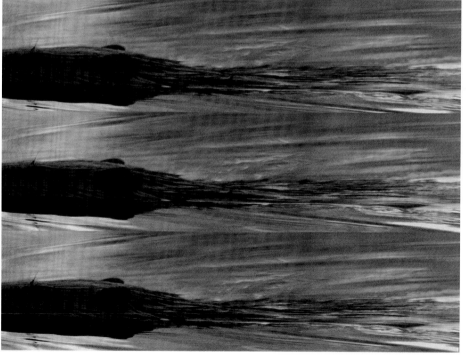

Dreams of Water Bodies

Wazhashk,
small whiskered swimmer,
you, a fluid arrow crossing waterways
with the simple determination
of one who has dived
purple deep into mythic quest.

Belittled or despised
as water rat on land;
hero of our Anishinaabeg people
in animal tales, creation stories
whose tellers open slowly,
magically like within a dream,
your tiny clenched fist
so all water tribes.
might believe.

See the small grains of sand—
Ah, only those poor few—
but they become our turtle island
this good and well-dreamed land
where we stand in this moment
on the edge of so many bodies of water
and watch *Wazhashk*, our brother,
slip through pools and streams and lakes
this marshland earth hallowed by
the memory
the telling
the hope
the dive
of sleek-whiskered-swimmers
who mark a dark path.

And sometimes in our water dreams
we pitiful land-dwellers
in longing
recall, and singing
make spirits ready
to follow:
*bakobii.***

*Nibii-wiiyawan Bawaadanan**

Wazhashk
agaashiinyi memiishanowed bagizod
biwak-dakamaadagaayin
mashkawendaman
googiigwaashkwaniyamban
dimii-miinaandeg gagwedweyamban.

Gigoopazomigoog
ninii-chiwaawaabiganoojinh akiing
ogichidaa Anishinaabe
awesiinaajimowinong, aadizookaanag
dash debaajimojig onisaakonanaanaawaa
nengaaj enji-mamaanjiding
gdobikwaakoninjiins
miidash gakina Nibiishinaabeg
debwewendamowaad.

Waabandan negawan
aah sa ongow eta
maaaji-mishiikenh-minis
minwaabandaan aakiing maampii
niigaanigaabawiying
agamigong
Wazhashk waabamang, niikaaninaanig
zhiibaasige zaaga'iganan gaye ziibiinsan
mashkiig zhawendang
mikwendang
waawiindang
ezhi-bagosendamowaad
ezhi-googiiwaad
agaashiinyag memiishanowewaad begizojig
dibiki-miikanong.

Nangodinong enji-nibii-bawaajiganan
gidimagozijig aakiing endaaying
bakadenodang
dash nagamoying
jiibenaakeying
noosone'igeying
bakobiiying.

7

*Translation by Margaret Noodin.   **Go down into the water.

Of Eons and Epics

i.
We wake with arrowheads—
our hands clamped around dreams,
dreams of hummocky bodies
glacial names tattooed
on each blue-rivered forearm.
What does it mean to hunger
for shards,
a glossary to story us?

I tell it this way:
the sculpting,
the whittle-form of earth—
say *kettle* with a hard *k*.
Something is always taken,
something left behind;
it becomes you—literally.
You tombolo, you esker.
We are all debris—
our story a remnant
of what moved across us.
What bounteousness!
We are glacial terrain,
marked pathways—myth.

What does it mean for my fingers, eyes, tongue?
to brim with a telling,
the silk-voiced dream
of one body moving against another?

ii.

Sometimes the story is simple:
the etched back of Turtle that holds us—
it asks only belief.
Earthdivers one and all—sleek
water bodies surfacing,
emerge to sing on holy ground.

But the way they tell it
we are land animals,
humanity a paradise of aloneness:
a solved mystery, a locked garden
a departure—
that story the walking away.
The way they tell it
the flood always recedes
from impossible watery origins.

But who fixes the science of meaning?
The truth is:
awake and asleep we betray our small selves
wander beyond borders—
is water bird a metaphor?

iii.

I tell it this way:
The diving for survival
(*mahng, amik, nigig*
together with mink and Nanaboozho).
Their feathered and furred bodies.
Ours. Gathering tiny grains of copper—
sand and sky's minstrel breath;
Noodin whirling from four directions,
until this:
small magic we call earth.
But feel the fire and flexing beneath us—
the rumble-voiced pulse of this planet,

the vibration of our tectonic bodies?
Remember, we too are still motion—
burning wet and storied,
mythic like Turtle Island.

Imagine with me metamorphic becoming,
each miraculous emergence:
tetrapod limbs
from gelatinous tadpole bodies,
oceans and islands
rising receding rising
in their dance with volcanic force.
Our lives, too, servant to the alchemy
to the carving gusts of wind and water,
time—and telling.

iv.
Sing me again the saga of sin
and separation,
of humans and hierarchies;
I'll sing you
the ballad of glacial bodies
of many creatures made of water and belief—
the one about transformations
about eons and epics—
these sacred cycles and everyday survivals.

The truth is:
we amphibious, we minstrel-born
wear the spiraling path of legends
on each whorled fingertip.
Like the trace of time on the clay of earth—
the drumlin swarms, the conical hills;
we too rise new each day from sleep
to storied lives—to archetypes and anthems,
to the spectacular castings of destiny.

Recite with me each rhapsody history or rumor—
our ancient epic inked now
pigment on rock-face, carbon on parchment,
memory on skin.

Please withhold koans and questions—about sound,

and each ageless clap of wave
on rock.
Here, too:
the simple destiny of seascape

a   s c a tter I n g   of   pixel

M o s a i c of light

silt   sand   shift
and sink.

Slippage

How many times lost
in the apparitions
of white dragon breath,
moon slipping in and out
behind the dancing fringe of fog?
Somewhere on the water's edge
trapped in the thin, horizon line
between dark-sky Thunderbirds
and legendary spiked sea serpents,
lonely souls yearn or keen
on too solid ground.
Finding the vaporous shore
where every solid thing
becomes unseen,
where water fills air,
and the great panther still roars
against the rocks.
Mishibijiw
summoner of the storms,
your tail a vision like copper,
riding the seiche and surge
sinking us, jagged and heavy as rock,
in the uncanny call of night.
Three quadrillion gallons of water—
never enough for escape.
Your lair deep, deeper. . .
1,333 icy deepest feet down,
past lost schooners, sunken freighters,
in the miasma of myth
where the Emperor and the Edmund Fitzgerald
now waltz together sweetly
in currents of *Gichigami*.
Each lost legend summoned
swallowed like the Nelson.

Submerged now, ship wheels still
then turn, the memory of squalls
bring splash and hiss echoing to shore
to wash the longing feet of wayfarers.
This ancient scented language
is sand, shells, and spray
the call of sea gulls and mystery,
is underwater monsters, craggy cliffs,
and, yes, our many drowned kingdoms.

Cadastre, Apostle Islands

i.
A soap-opera rising and sinking of bodies,
melt of glaciers, flamboyant sculpture of waves—
west wind at thirty knots—
this serial archipelago the drama of centuries.
Forgotten Steamboat Island
swallowed like the sunken ships—
one episode of tide and time,
now another buried underwater treasure.
How to plat the ancient—*27,232 submerged acres*;
mark or name the temporary—newly formed seastacks,
shifting sand spits and tombolos?

Imagine the geared toy of evolution:
twenty-two islands swimming in *40 degrees*, in aqua,
honeycombed with vaulted chambers, with caverns
whose deeply carved crevices house whisper
and splash, echo cormorant and eagle scree
(breeding habitat for 150 bird species)
harbor the keening of human loss—
distress signals at 2:05 a.m..
How to measure this littoral expanse—man miles or
decibels of the surf drum on mythic Devils isle?

Imagine henna wheat copper buff and umber arches—
where layered sandstone rises red and cathedral gothic
at *Swallow's Point, Mawikwe Bay.*
Yes, each epoch a burnished stratum, a wave of color.
We flat map with metes and bounds—*Manitou Island,*
Hermit, Ironwood—trace ownership in treaties and deeds,
but cannot account each mystic transformation:
the graceful circumference of wind twists in white pine,
or how the friction of time and waves shape song—
emitted frequency 450 Hertz.

My feet a plectrum on the quartz lyre of Stockton Island
this globular singing sand is nature's genius,
the whistle, squeak, or eerie bark—ephemeral.

ii.

Beyond flat fact Apostle Island histories overlap, stack
like horse skeletons at the bottom of each ravine:
the glimpse of steamer spines in clear water,
the sunken and mummified hemlock and birds-eye maple—
salvage logs now kilned and carved to fine-grained guitars.
The past is hollow bellies of Anishinaabeg canoes
is the echo of old names and the weighted fill of rocks—
birch bark given to winter waters for preservation.
The piled stone, the stories—*Midewiwin lodges,*
Voyageurs and fisheries, lighthouses and loggers—
trace another measure, paint the palimpsest of place.

Among abandoned brownstone quarries on Basswood Island
each cubed hollow the math of absence and distance—
of *courthouse buildings* rising square by brown square
in mainland cities like Bayfield and Milwaukee.
This beanstalk-tall barter is also loss:
of peerless brown furs
traded to drape bodies of moneyed matrons,
or *500 million board feet* of disappearing timber each year.
When history is a bedlam of *John Jacob Astor* commodity
and weather a storied purple destiny of ships run aground,
who can name island gods or number sands on *Raspberry,*
Otter, Gull, and Oak?
How ruler each breathless angel edge
of ledge rock, record equation for velocity of change,
mirror the fetal scroll of fiddlehead ferns—
or praise with proper song each turtle-shaped survival?

Angles of Being

It's all angle after all. What we see and especially what we miss.

Like the leaf bird limed and shadowed, a match to every other green upturned hand blooming on the August tree. Indecipherable. Even when wings flutter like leaves in breeze.

Or the silhouette—dark and curved on the bare oak. Beak, parted tail, each mistakable for knot, branch, or twig. Only when one exits the scene, unblends and isolates itself, flies against too blue sky does the game of hidden pictures end.

Ah, angles. Tell all or tell it slant. What we dream, appear, or inverted seem to be.

Talking Rock

i.

Oak wilt. A trench cut to prevent spread. And the rocks that tumble like rosetta stones from the turned earth. In this playground of soft soil as the dogs nose and dig, I crouch among the buried. Fingers fumble over scores and hollows in stone. How to read each story? Hear each tiny ochre voice?

ii.

I remember three *manidoog* brothers, the last a stone. *Maskasaswabik.*
Two brothers wandered hunting, craving adventure. At camp, Stone waited.
Trickster *Naanabozho* plotted to kill the brother that anchored him.
Failed with borrowed axe. Only Stone himself knew how he could be broken.
Yes, he told. Hot fire, cold water. A rock body shattering multiplies.
In thousands of pieces he now ranges the earth. Poor peripatetic *Naanabozho*
can never travel beyond where his Stone brother lies.

iii.

Like petroforms, the smallest pebbles we touch carry history from another place, a different time. And, like an ancient one startled awake, these talking rocks continue their tale. *Ah, Trickster, lives doomed, his fate like his relative Sisyphus. You see him now—a relentless rock hound, compelled to collect and assemble the pieces of his mischief. To gather the remnants of his shattered stone sibling, all the while carrying the worthless pick-axe.*

iv.

Now sift. What the dogs unmask. Rock bodies. Fossils. Remnants of small forms who have secreted themselves ages ago. At my caress they whisper being. I lift story, solid as stone.

Pica

Eat the upside down Vs of forest ∧∧∧∧,
each small stuttering - - - - dash of rustic roads.
My pedals devour miles; my shaded eyes,
names: Big Foot Beach, Devil's Lake.
The taste of mythology on my tongue,
this cartographic hunger. Now tip
the tiny cups ∪∪∪∪∪∪ of lakes
the blue spilling veins of ancient rivers.
Pause for fill at each crisscross view
++++ of bridges, of tattered railways
vanishing into planted fields of forever.
Inhale lingering scent of wild on onion—
this papyrus, this map of belonging.

Winter Transfigurations

after *Skating in Central Park*, Agnes Tait, 1934

i.

In Wisconsin winter, fields stretch out and endlessly
white keeps falling on white.
Suddenly one morning the snow is spotted with dark bodies,
the sky strung with migrating waterfowl
returning, geese sit huddled
honking into late winter storms,
while beaks of sandhill cranes lift like praying hands,
and mallards gather where day by day ice returns to water.
Beyond calendar and almanac, a cold waiting—
and feathered instincts like faith.

ii.

On Central Park's winter slopes and frozen pond
an idyll of Americana, 1930's diorama laced with colorful animation
where a bounty of outstretched limbs race the fleeing day.
Beyond the sight of Hoovervilles, backlit by golden sky
sled follows sled, cap to boot down the slope—
skinny-legged mutts a blur of bark and chase.
Now center stage, a jumble of skaters set their blades, push off
hands linked like cut-out dolls. Yes, on tingling legs
they lean and push and lean and build a holy
speed until they whirl themselves forward
slant forms following a frozen arc   a rhapsody
of flushed bodies moving clockwise and counter, becoming
on the other side of ice, a silver memory of color—
finally called from glistening mirage by
matrons and bonnet-headed babies.

In depression era New York, misted layers of faded skyline waver:
a grey city drop cloth, artist's outline of fabled civilization sinking
into darkness, while evening exiles follow arabesque patterns
across the footbridge, breathe the soft dove call of forgetfulness,

enter a comforting circle of twinkling lights and woodland sentinels.
Here tree trunks delicately ink themselves on every surface:
a nest of intricate lines tattoo the island hill
bare brush anchors rocks and bronze-coated watchers
branches extend into the damp steam of encroaching dusk.
Until in the fairy-tale of this imaginary forest
the simple bent lines of limbs and bodies become labyrinth.
Silhouettes— dog, skater, tree—overlap and tangle
indistinguishable, all nothing but leaning energy
each a dark digit, a tally in the ancient sum of hopefulness.

iii.

As March days grow longer, flock by flock they arrive
song birds taking their directions from night stars,
geese tracking dramatic Vs across spring skies.
Air carries migratory signals, territorial claims, mating calls—
elaborate refrains part the grey air of winter silence.
Birds perch on hummocks, brave icy waterways,
or congregate in tree tops to lustily sing their survival.
In the slowly darkening farmlands they peck expectantly
at still-hardened ground and wander fields like hungry refugees:
each fragile body rehearsing ritual and expectation—
mastering the simple art of enduring.

After Taiwan

I watch the umbrella tip walk slowly up the Erzihping Trail and the deep
scarlet fleece at the woman's waist swing slightly side to side, unfurling like
a conquering flag. One step ahead, a navy backpack bounces just below her
husband's abundant grey hair. Now the tall grasses of Mount Datun rise on
each side of the figures, closing around them as they diminish into smaller
and smaller memory.

They wanted a photo. Their ancient everyday. My foreign face. In the digital
window where we stand together in the Tamsui morning, my wide smile
reflects the joy I feel in their presence. Eighty. Still hiking. In tandem.
I imagine the island years, the long sequence of suns. Like this January orb
that warms my shoulders. Or later plays so generously across the tiles at Tian
Yuan. Showing to perfect effect the temple's scores of brilliant dragons, the
wall of hungry tigers.

What we found in the mountain morning: No serow, wild boar, Formosan
sambar. No clouded leopard or any of the other twenty-eight mammal
species. Many are rare, endangered. Some have not been sighted for years,
may already have gone with the older suns.

Not so the stone lions who welcome visitors and guard the temple grounds.
Not so the extravagant tropical flowers in fiery palettes, the sweet-scented
incense sticks, the overflowing bowls of ripe fruit presented at altars. Not so
the simple solemnity of bowing before good.

After Taiwan, I wondered at the artist's way. With a wealth of words or
watercolors, what to place in the foreground, what receding at the edge of
vision?

Caption

This is not a photograph of the woman inside the house.
This is not even the door to the quiet room where she lies,
more quiet still. No, this is a waboose, a wild spring creature,
its nose twitching in a way the camera cannot show. A rabbit
that has come for the dew, the dew on the grass outside the house
that is not pictured here. A rabbit who will feast on the garden
that is still in seed, the garden that will grow plants wild
like the waboose. The garden that will belong to the rabbit
and will not be hoed by the woman who is not pictured here.

Words on Yearning

We wake
tiny in the panorama.
in the ancient curves of earth:
grey arch and steeple of stone, green tango
swoop of valley, spires of redwoods,
these postcard layers—
holy endlessness.

Paint with plaintive voice,
a prayer,
a hunger for sorting.
The strata, this knowing:
like papery reeds rising
over the aqua unreality of lake water
over shore bugs
over shale and flint
(over bedrock, sandstone, and dolomite).

A science of taxonomy.

But this unnamed, unnameable—
brim of the before and after.

Life bodies a mere vibration.

Song of crane
over cattail
over and over green;

and solid earth spilling itself
into blue,
river horizon
becoming sky.

Each patchwork tier the color of transience.

Each patchwork tier the color of transience.

Who can number the arched back of shadows
dancing on hills,
spell the motion of glaciers
the changeling forms of land masses?

Simply rise now
in your small yearning.

Face the ancient wash:
waters a ripple of copper light
at dawn, at dusk—
this blessed flame ageless.
Know the hot lick of shifting colors:
skies purpling into night.

A mind that lifts
song to this lode.

A word tether of seamlessness.

An ageless yearning—to sleep within.

II.

HUNGER
FOR BALANCE

Of Fractals and Pink Flowering

(after Eric and Heather ChanSchatz "The Next Generation")

Imagine the geometry of flower
is hunger for balance,
is my child's hand on the gears of beauty
layering and interlocking color.
Picture me prone, a small center point—
one copper dot in the white Minnesota winter.
Picture my mother drying her hands
placing the compass and spinning
arcs and intersecting curves,
woodland flowers growing
into many-petaled mandalas
into limitlessness: a universe
of circles, of symmetry—sun,
stars, blooms and orange-hued fruits,
the berry, squash, ripe tomato wonder
of belonging.

            My own spirograph bursts
rush forth ornate like paisley, like fireworks
against dark summer sky. Spokes and wheels
and gears meshing—each pencil thrust
a tentative mark, a hopeful threading
of the cogs of longing. Imagine my fingers
holding tight to the friction,
watch the intricate flourishes appear
on white paper—the tabula rasa
transformed by oval,
just another language
another voice saying hello
to the spiraling bodies of self.

Imagine my psychedelic crayola
yearning, my January pining
after the purple florals
the cosmos, the daisy mix
(he loves me, he loves me not)
on Gurney's seed packs.
Now watch as we carve splendor:
my world is medicine wheel and hand drum,
is pow-wow bustle and beadwork in woodland design.
The sweep of nature tallied by curve,
by eye, assembled now as scarlet fractals,
as collage of vines, tassels, seed pods,
and a child's simple pink infinity.

This Stranger's Beauty

Barely formed fetus feet and tiny Spock ears
Ripley's surreal—this listing on the edge of small perfection;
pink mouse pup bald and suckling blindly from the doe
feeding as we all do on the driven milk of becoming.

Somewhere beneath the sealed lumps of black eyes
a swimming to awareness under the stretched membrane of skin,
you a mere half gram and every pore and wrinkle a vanity
of knowing your own ghostly poetry, your fragility.

Everywhere we look—whimsy and a holy clamor for survival:
wolf spiderlings cling like moss to their mother's back
while guppies and even angelfish gulp their fry
and still my lonely violin heart tunes to frog song,

to wolf howl and loon calls and other darker matter.
I believe in the fluid arch of frill-necked lizards,
impossible serrated swirls, like cirque de soleil
Seeker's eels. All a reptilian anti-splendor—*the horror.*

The heart of darkness illuminated by small gods
or blind and relentless human hunger for beauty,
as if each striped haunch and stretch were our own
each turquoise spot the simple reversal of revulsion.

We know contortion of birth, our own grotesque
sad embrace of air, of gravity. The slither and purple weight
of voice, the awakening flex of body. Hold this strange light—
a relentless spilling of fever over the untrammelled earth.

Dreams of Water Bodies, Two

Like the alchemy of sun and water
your motion that quicksilver
flash, body a dark shining,
sleek, only a ripple passing
over rock at the edge of vision,
or a pouring of black body
endlessly, a ribbon of liquid
grace, exhilaration, river
otter.

Tethered by infatuation
I pursue down narrow streams.
Scanning, expectation, each glimpse an elixir,
an awakening, like movement itself.
And in the momentum of arms
paddling kayaks paddling canoes paddling
moments, each water craft glides on.
Now you turn, bold and black, head then chin lifts—
twinkle of your look, of mine.

Again you dive, tip of your tail
a single black quotation mark
opening a conversation
for which I've found no end.
Having followed for years water clues
bubbles you've left in your wake
slight lines across glassy surfaces
ever watchful for signal, tiny chirp
that tempts me off the map.

The game is all chase, tease and slide.
But soon trolling black bodies secret themselves
in lodges, there murmur and grunt.
This river language enchanting, hypnotic, lulls me

as the sun and I lean, too, and linger at rest.
Until one day I tie the canoe, drape myself
like a turtle on a rock to watch and wait
as time itself laps laps at all finite edges
rocks, dens, otters—and me.

Then the alchemy of sun and water calls
me a dark shining, above or below
the surface, dreams of water bodies
limitless in their motion, a ribbon
shimmering silver, thundersky blue, thinning
infinitesimal line passing amphibious between realms,
amid murmured prayers: adoramus and Old Heaven,
keep your trumpets, send me rivered grace
pour me anew into this blackswimming waterspirit.

BWCA Haiku

Eerie wisps of white
stir the damp air at daylight—
ghost mists on Pine Lake.

Morning lake a mirror
sandpiper bends to water
brown beak meets brown beak.

Trio of blueberries
glistens on morning ledge rock,
paddler's reward.

Iron cold and wild
a million wet blue acres;
drink in your smallness.

Across endless dark
echoing calls, wolf and loon—
fluid song of night.

What I Believe

after Michael Blumenthal

I believe the weave of cotton
will support my father's knees,
but no indulgences will change hands.

I believe nothing folds easily,
but that time will crease—
retrain the mind.

I believe in the arrowheads of words
and I believe in silence.

I believe the rattle of birch leaves
can shake sorrow from my bones,
but that we all become bare at our own pace.

I believe the songs of childhood
follow us into the kettles of age,
but the echoes will not disturb the land.

I believe the reach of the kayak paddle
can part the blue corridor of aloneness,
and that eyes we see in water are never our own.

A Litany of Other

i.

My doppelaganger self,
she knows the slight weight
of a folded twenty,
knows how to smooth Andrew Jackson
bend and turn him, origami the Indian-war president
to a tucked and folded three-cornered retired flag neatness.
Then, holding him, a triangle of envy green, centered in her palm,
knows the precise pitch of lip
necessary to win each bar-stool happy-hour wager.
My doppelaganger self
wears river blue to match his eyes
and never worries
it doesn't flatter her complexion.
Yes D knows her way around the longings
of saddle-sore five o'clock gamblers.
Don't bet against her—
with lace, she could have changed history.

ii.

Watch that plaid skirt betray her
pitiful doppelganger self, uniformed and crepe-shoed.
She nicely pitched her story
smelled the sweet tobacco victory,
almost talked herself into a new job, new car,
new persona, new paperback eternity.
But damn that sinful hunger for piety,
that doppelganger mission-school purity;
modest slip beneath the skirt—
her wardrobe malfunction
will never make the tabloids.
Destiny laughs at my doppelganger self
using words like autonomy;
no self-made woman here it snarls,

no sharp-heeled feminine foot on snakeskin.
Iron the simple white blouse, don the Clark Kent glasses,
save your Green Stamps, and wait little D, wait
perhaps understated retro will circle back in time.

iii.

That doppelganger turning over in her sleep,
spying the silver—shaped like wolf, like moonlight,
that pajama-clad nightshade woman who pads slipperless
to the window yawning into another reality,
climbs through and doesn't look back,
that sweet hungry wry fearless beauty
who rows through the dark on Vermilion Lake
could never be my morning-breath-mouthwash self,
except for the one night I tumbled through gardens
weaving down echoing alleys in summer sandals,
carrots spilling out my every crevice.
That girl was neither scarecrow nor common garden thief,
but dark and hungry nymph, a minor god of indiscretion.
I've loved her when I was sure no one was watching—
me spiraling through time on trains in foreign cities,
with her face just outside the smeared window glass.
When you slide down the slope of another body
who can decipher the warmer half?

iv.

Alone, I've unpacked her doppelganger smile,
gently shook it out, and tried it on. Before the mirror
I am D, am me—transforming to the million digits of pi
and beyond. The crow outside your window
watching you black and raven like Poe's own haunting.
Do we envy them their otherness?
Their not always predictable me-ness?
She saunters in, my doppelganger self
I dress her in my still-tagged, never-worn pieces of self.
Who knows who we might have been in another life?
Could be in the Russian-dolls hidden inside inside inside—

empty bodies abandoned like cicada shells, only husks
of dry remembering while molted and winged
doppelgangers shed our languid one-dimensional song.
The treble-clef hair of my doppelganger self
swinging out behind, following her around each corner
each corner the one where I almost catch her tuber words.

What the Rain Remembers

Walk hostage, and wait:
somewhere summer and thunder
will spill truth. Crinkled corn stalks
will talk, cicadas friction their voices.
The patter of sun showers on every water surface—
a musical code.

Memorize the tiny glyph of bird feet,
the ancient braille of the pileated woodpecker.
Each ecofact a sign or pattern. Everywhere
beneath the dust of human passing—a secret.

Mold from earth's clay a talisman.
Walk backwards by fours.

And when the skies again break
us open and filling like rivers,
who knows what flat and buried lies—
the mythic wash of rain may bare.

Becoming Turtle

Coffee and I waiting
while spatterdock nods
softly, and yellow dots
  dance above
          dance below the surface
as wake of our passing
ripples   ripples   and settles.

Kayak nestled now
deep in marsh morning,
quiet and waiting waiting
for birds to return to cattail perches
to take up their song,
for turtles to seek the sun,
muskrats to emerge and circle
warily wondering.

Wondering as I do
if I am motion or rock,
floating on the surface

or sunk now
dreaming in watery words.

Tincture

The shaft of your eye catching the reflected light of these Minnesota lakes—
Bad Medicine, Height of Land, Sugarbush, South Twin, White Earth—a long
sequence of wet bodies beneath bobbers, of dark eyes squinting into sunlight,
into green depths. The flash of your vision a replica of the striking bass,
white-scaled belly turning in the reeds. The movement there says everything
that must be said.

I lift the net. You point your chin. The fish dives and your pole bows
as if in politeness. We gesture, dance lightly across years.

And I thought reflection timeless.

But it dims.

Another Intimation

for Amy

Spendthrift fall
recklessly spilling seed,
pods, leaves, bodies—and I
a lush
as if color
as if you.
Now each tiny eye
in the cottony
reach
of milkweed
totters—
a debutante on display.
Ah, spin lightly
in autumn's dance,
that copper-hued gesture
mnemonic as melody,
as the simple sun we hum.

Endaso-Dagwaagin

Here Chickadees flutter to rice—
tiny balls of flesh and feather
their high-pitched *dee-dee-dee*
sharp like fall's pine-edged
echoing air.
Birds shoot up, like green needles
thrust skyward into endlessness,
like days rising into a lake-blue forever.
Now September winds rustle branches
sway the tiny ripe heads
the brown the russet the gold.
Until the black-capped gatherers
burst from high branches and swoop
swallow-swift, bodies elongated
in a stream of movement—
wild like the oats
they seek.

This watcher's heart flutters, too
with the spectral blur of speed
or some memory
simple and satisfying.
Something repeated—songbirds
or destiny.
Like we who move between the colors
marking the air
with sounds.
Earth garments ring bold and joyous at the harvest:
the chanting woods, tamarac stands and sumac,
pine cones scattered and full to bursting.
Woods that wait still in the sight of other gatherers
those callers after birds
whose brown hands also
hovered over ripe grains.

The motion of *manoomin*
in fall, the color of ripeness,
seed and seed gatherers
in *dagwaagin*:
this season is bird calls in copper
the song of something old and swift—
time or the wings that move
fluttering like sprites.
The season belongs to chickadee birds
and to watchers who luxuriate and linger
in golden forests
while days shorten and grow cool
shorten and grow
into echoes of old songs
shorten and grow
into poems
of recollection.

Manoominike-giizis

Ricing moon
when poling arms groan
like autumn winds through white pine.
Old rhythms find the hands
bend and pound the rice,
rice kernels falling
falling onto wooden ribs
canoe bottoms filling with memories—
new moccasins dance the rice
huffs of spirit wind lift and carry the chaff
blown like tired histories
from birchbark winnowing baskets.
Now numbered
by pounds, seasons, or generations
lean slivers of parched grain
settle brown and rich
tasting of northern lakes
of centuries.

III.

FRAYED
HISTORIES

A Subjectifixation Cento for Two Voices*

Littered with the detritus
of what we are under a lens,

Indians are not clean.

in empty territories
claimed Terra Nuluis
by greedy men,

They are unGodly and ignorant,

the latch
is the small hook and eye
of religion.

with a bestiary for a family album.

it is not what you imagine,
no matter what you imagine—

Pitch devils.

this cage of flesh and bone
needs cleaning.

In this age called America,
we can eat their spirits like corn

My touch is a history book
full of lies and half-forgotten truths,

Indians are like children.

colonial genealogies.

dependent upon the Queen mother.

I am the historical schizophrenia
of beadwork and jewelry and lost languages.

Try to forget this pagan tongue.

written by others
who hold the pens and the power.

*Think and remember what happens
to girls who speak a pagan tongue*

The arrest of a woman
in long black tresses

Timber niggerr.

whose hysterical laughter
caused a public nuisance.

*Stray bullets—the only good Indian
is a dead one.*

All graves are pregnant with our nearest kin.

* All language in the poem comes from the poetry of Anishinaabe writers collected in
Traces in Blood, Bone, and Stone: Contemporary Ojibwe Poetry.

Of Nalusachito and the Course of Rivers

for Louis

I would have gone to him then—in the lost river.
The character who lived haunting the edge,
his keen raw in the night, a scream decades loud—
the mixedblood scream that opens us.
Like male rain always falling in the stories
streaming myth and planting seeds of shadows.
Those dark and true near beings, who lean
always a whisper step away—kin to desire.
How long this dark cast of shadow, bodies
emptied of light; this dry bed of absence, waters
a remnant disappearing from sight? No measure
for this—for us, beneath the patient moon.

Such shapes, not figment nor pacing shade
of panther—but the thin pen of hunger
hunting names stolen, erased, buried. Half-forgotten
half-remembered. Bifurcated. But refusing each
printed erasure: treaties, maps, formulas—
complicated calculations, destiny in degrees.
Here inscribe soul math, of latitude and blood.
Yes, I would unbury the bones of story
lie down beside them in nameless river bottoms,
rivers dried and waiting for Thunder
those beings of myth and copper-laced ether,
those harbingers—those Ancients.

Lie with me, bleached now of hope and rage.
Eyes lifted, whetted—like the fracture of your face
against certain slants of sky. This telling crow simple;
not the caricature of invented skin we shed
(shed and shed and burn like soiled clothing).
Remember: *This river—the dried tongue.*
The bones abandoned here. The rains that come.
A plot more jagged than gothic: death, panther, river
—me. What I become outside the measure
of savage remnant, of dime-novel, of fantasy.
An other epic, storied now in bark, in rattle
song of thunder, in paper echo: the recycled
telling of half breed—now turned whole.

Verse Drama One: Pagan

Don't preach me reward.
I have seen the skin maps leading there.
Who burned our homes, our crops
pointed us toward earth's promised land
now tells of heaven's.
Sit here belief and warm yourself
these fires made by hands not devils.

Verse Drama Two: Surveyor, 1849

Somewhere in the middle
of naming greatness
one nation tumbled
into the waters of history
or into the deep end
of an unfamiliar mythic pool
where lakeness too
finds something resembling
itself a semblance
brought about by
dissembled fragments
of assembled desire
in other words
someone son of hugh
or frankly
perhaps
a river himself
turned story
into some
thing simpler
chart or name:
mendota.

Rattle

I fold the ghost of paper *of peace and friendship*
gently as if words could break,
tuck it *final and binding* inside my muklaks
hidden now beneath my feet.

Feet, windows of the soul,
souls lost in that history,
history a banquet
without enough chairs.

I take the pemmican, treaty whiskey,
the pipe. Still sacred.
I relative of all X marks.
fold the ghost of paper *obligatory upon the Indians.*

Thin stick syllables of deceit
the second clause of the second article,
voices of spine and serif
hereunto set their hands and affixed their seals.

Blood smear of hollow promises
this dream paper inked
or etched like scars on skin
redskin. *Hereby ceded.*

Forget the treaty—*privilege of hunting,*
fishing, and gathering the wild rice—
old history they tell me:
excepting the reservations made and described.

In their ears trees don't rattle
rattle haunted with copper longing.
The folded paper, ghost of folded life:
pursuits of civilized—a sheaf in capture code.

1850. Sandy Lake, Minnesota.

An evil Wiindigoo. Ramsey schemed
Re   m o v a l
lured tribal leaders—
money promises
&
dangled annuities.

"You shall have plenty to eat and be fat and I will make your payment quick."

19 bands
3,000 Ojibwe
rendezvous and wait—

Binaakwe-giizis/Falling Leaves Moon
Gashkadino-Giizis/Freezing Moon
Manidoo-Giizisoons/Little Spirit Moon.

"We went, but did not find him there."

Living on BIA lies bodies fail:
in hunger
in crowded makeshift camps
tribes wait for contaminated food,
for measles, dysentery, and starvation
for undelivered annuity payments
for the dark tally—
170
die waiting for Ramsey's plenty.

"We saw the ground covered with the graves of our children and relatives."
"Graves were to be seen in every direction, for miles distant, from Sandy Lake."

We called it "the Burying Place."

In mourning,
cheated by the tardy agent,
yearning faces turn toward home.

Trade blankets to feed their remaining children.

"The rivers had frozen and we had to throw away our canoes
and go to our distant homes with our families on foot."

One more nineteenth century death march—
just another check mark in a colonial ledger book:

weak with parceled out hunger
traveling hundreds of miles to
Wisconsin,
Michigan,
northern Minnesota

through winter snow, through freezing temperatures—

"Their food was all gone. . . . They came on . . .
bringing the dead bodies of their children on their backs."

Count them:
the bodies wrapped in bark
left behind in shallow graves
the silent babies carried home—

400 Ojibwe ancestors lost
on the Chippewa Trail of Tears.

Mochi, Prisoner of War

Remember her in winter. Picture her as she was then in Black Kettle's camp. A young woman of 24. Southern Cheyenne, of the Tse Tse Stus band. In the tipi of her parents.

Remember her at Fort Marion. Imprisoned with her warrior husband Chief Medicine Water. The infamous Captain Richard Pratt her warden.

Try to imagine the slow-motion-minutes that changed her life: Dawn. November 29, 1864. You are Mochi—Buffalo Calf. Your band is camped at Big Sandy Creek. Your leader Black Kettle flies America's stars and stripes above his lodge. Flies the white flag of truce. You are safe here and Black Kettle has sent the warriors to hunt buffalo.

This is United States History 101. Fact: Black Kettle's peaceful camp is not safe. Mochi is not safe. Indians in colonial America cannot be safe. Fact: U.S. Army Colonel John Chivington was a Methodist preacher. He was a freemason and opponent of slavery. Chivington, however, was not an opponent of murdering Indians.

You are Mochi in winter camp with your mother. It is dawn when your life explodes around you. The first explosion is the bullet entering your mother's forehead. The second explosion comes as you fight off the soldier attempting to rape you. You have made that explosion with your grandfather's rifle and the soldier falls. You run then into the chaos and through the cannon fire and the screaming and the slashed and disemboweled bodies.

Imagine your life now as a long series of explosions and escapes. You are Mochi the warrior, the raider. Imagine you remember the explosions when you sleep. You see the soldiers each time you raise your rifle. Kill the memories over and over for eleven long years. Exploding them and running from them, until finally you surrender at Fort Leavenworth.

Remember her in winter. Picture her as she was then in Black Kettle's camp. Remember her at Fort Marion. Imprisoned with her warrior husband Chief Medicine Water.

Text books call it Chivington's massacre; but Sand Creek was also Mochi's spiritual transformation. Let us call her Mochi the witness, the survivor. Prisoner of War.

Estate of Chief Black Kettle (1813-1868)

That we may not be mistaken by them for enemies.
Motavato (Black Kettle), autumn, 1864

Peace medal from Abraham Lincoln

34-star American flag presented by Colonel Greenwood—flown over his tipi to stave off attack

White flag of truce

Appointment as Chief in the Cheyenne Council of Forty-four

Official papers declaring him a "good friend" of the United States

Treaty at Fort Laramie.

Treaty at Fort Wise.

Peace settlement at Fort Weld.

"Perpetual Peace" in the Treaty of Little Arkansas River

Medicine Lodge Treaty.

Title of "Peace Chief"

Livestock: 21 horses and 6 mules—valued by U.S. at $1,425.00 after their destruction at Sand Creek

Nine bullets removed from his wife Medicine Woman Later after the Sand Creek Massacre

A rally of bullets to the back while retreating at Washita River

Portrayed as "good Indian" in television's *Dr. Quinn, Medicine Woman*

Memorial at Black Kettle National Grassland

Sutra, in Umber

November, 2009. In gracious remnants of fall sun, my hair warms to its roots.
Now, silent as heat, deer materialize amid columns of Fort Snelling oak,
recede again into weathered wood. We walk with uncertain ghosts.

Here is old Dakota Territory. A confluence of rivers, a mythic place of origin.
Makoce Cokaya Kin. Where the Minnesota meets the Mississippi. Center of
the Earth. Here, too, 1600 Dakota women, children, and heartbroken old men
became prisoners. Interred on these grounds.

I pass like breath into the hollow, slowly move among the deer. In the
stillness of intrusion time falls away. On the ground of trampled leaves, in
a light of indistinguishable origin, I remember the story. Imagine the way
history sinks into sepia.

Winter, 1862. Starvation and disease here beneath the trees. The Dakota
camp already overcrowded—occupied by the dark specter of murder.
Memories of thirty-eight warrior bodies swing like pendulums on the colonial
metronome. Mass execution. Each day until May more Dakota spirits slip
away, step into dusky rumors about vanished heathens. 300 prisoners never
leave these grounds.

Spring enters amid vacant-eyed strangers. Steamboats churn sacred waters.
And survivors again leave their homelands, their relatives, their dead. Passing
into exile. Before me now longing fills the forest like dew. Each burr, each
blade of bister grass remembers. And soon every black bark knot becomes
eyes.

I tell myself only the deer live here now. Glimpse their branch antlers curved,
leaf ears erect. But in this wavering between one being and another, in the
vital shimmer of unknowing, I see the tree bark faces of the many sentient.
Earth—the simple ink-trace of ancients. As if story and landscape converge.
Forever inseparable.

Summary Tabulations Descriptive of One Hundred and Fifty Chippewa Indian Families on the White Earth Reservation*

1938.
An anthropologist in Ojibwe country
black-robed and wimpled,
Mary Inez, you cast yourself among tribal clans.
Summer and fall you study count calculate and tally:
religious affiliations, the liquor problem,
housing conditions, retention of the Chippewa language,
household equipment, unmarried mothers.
size and use of rooms—
in appendices and tables you set your faith.
Outside White Earth lakes lap mildly
amidst tamaracks and the graceful bow of white birch,
close among the call of checker-backed loons
whose vowel song ripples the blue edges of eternity.
Methodically, you collect data on doors:
find *inside doors* absent in *44 homes.*
find *99 homes* with *unscreened outside doors.*
Carefully you accumulate details of floor coverings:
count *8 traditional bulrush mats,*
79 braided rag rugs of six or eight ply.
Sister, with pink Lady Slippers opening at your feet
how can you march booted and laced among the columns
and lead-pencil precision of mathematical statistics?
Dutifully you kneel to ruler, record
Smallest tar-paper shack, 630 total cubic feet of airspace,
Largest tar-paper shack, 5940 total cubic feet of airspace.
But who will chart the indigo fathoms of tribal lakes
assign measure, cube or square moving wings across migizi skies
pencil numbers on noodin, ancient breath of chanting ogichidaa?
And if you do not count each tinkling silver cone
worn on the dream-born jingle dress in June,
how can you believe you calculate culture?

* All italicized words are taken from Sister M. Inez Hilger's *Chippewa Families: A Social Study of White Earth Reservation, 1938.*

Ancient Hunger

> *From which tree does the cicada's shrill cry come?*
> —Zhāng Dàqiān

There—
backlit from the sun.
hair thin as embroidery floss,
blown like etch-a-sketch lines
across the shadow
of half-remembered features—
this impalpable.

Unnamed moss voices,
some bark ridge of story.
Always this swaying
beyond my ken,
before the tablet of knowing.
Each sound a ripple,
the aching edge of a cicada's call.

Does some child self linger
there beneath the limber strands of the willow tree?
Oh! the long low stretch of green—
leafy fringe of the mesmerizing circle.
Bending now, I search again
tabernacle of abandoned hopes
one side of the sanctum, the other.
I've gathered years of glimpses—
this muse.

Captivity

i.

A mark across the body. The morning I watched my beloved uncle disappear
down the alley. His car left sitting in our yard for 30 days. This tattoo
we cover with shame. The stories my mother whispered as if *gitchi-manidoo*
was a child who should not be told of the troubles of humans. All those taken.
Visits made on dusty trains. Letters adorned like birch bark art with lines
and tiny holes. My shriveled grandma "an accessory" hiding my cousin
from the interchangeable uniforms of civil pursuit. Her white hair another
flag of truce.

ii.

This is how we look over our shoulder. This is how we smile carefully in public
places. This is how we carry our cards, our identities. This is how we forget—
and how you remind us.

iii.

Mary Rowlandson made it big in the colonial tabloids. Indian captivity
narrative a seeming misnomer. But ink makes strong cultural bars of bias.
This is how we remain captured in print.

iv.

Now I harbor fugitive names. ██ c sin came to my reading in ankle tether.
Qu █i chained herself before the R █C█ building in protest. M █cus who
cannot receive email. The Ar█t█c█at manager from Thi█f█ive█ ls. His
whiskey-inspired stories tell of cicada existence—a cyclical shedding of
"dangerous" identities.

v.

We molt. The shell of our past a transparent *chanhua*. Yes, we will eat it
like medicine.

IV.

ALCHEMY
INHERITED

On Climbing Petroglyphs

i.

Newly twelve with size seven feet
dangling beside mine off the rock
ledge, legerdemain of self knowledge.
How do I say anything—magic
words you might need to hear?
With flute-playing, green-painted nails
your child's fingers reach to span the range
of carmel-colored women in our past.
Innocently you hold those ghost hands:
each story a truce we've made with loss.
How can I tell you there were others?

Big-boned women who might try
to push out hips in your runner's body.
Women who will betray you for men,
a bottle, or because they love you
love you, don't want to see you disappointed
in life, so will hold you, hold you hostage
with words, words tangled around courage
duty or money. When should I show you
my own flesh cut and scarred on the barbs
of belonging and love's oldest language?

ii.

No, let us dangle here yet, dawdle
for an amber moment while notes shimmer
sweetly captured in turquoise flute songs—
the score of a past we mark together.
No words whispered yet beyond these painted
untainted rock images of ancients: sun, bird, hunter.
Spirit lines that copper us to an infinity.
Endurance. Your dangling. Mine.
Before the floor of our becoming.
Perhaps even poets must learn silence,
that innocence, that space before speaking.

Veteran's Day

In the blaze orange of autumn
tall marsh grasses lie flattened.

Close here where deer will bed
I bend, sniff, search for other sign.

This safety where I too have sheltered
cast in the hollow of other lives.

Burst milkweed pods spill white
and burrs cling like unrecited prayers.

Hunter's air taunt now with expectation,
and cardinal, too, wearing Christmas red

for protection, as some crisp fear lingers
ever at the edge of boot steps and finite vision.

This earth will always vibrate with absent names
called in autumn and scented with gun shot.

In glacial kettles old grasses reseed each season:
where deer bed, some like wolves will wait.

Fire, After Fire

Evening's amber light among the lily pads. We paddle the narrow pathways of Pagami Creek. Still-charred trees lean against a perfect August sky, as if held up by the very clouds. At every turn—fireweed. Hills flaming scarlet, whisper to me a secret about survival.

I picture mad crown fires. All that has burned in our lives: Sacred sites. Subversive books. I think of all "noble" causes and their aftermath. Each scorched earth campaign.

But here is nature's cycle: A lightning strike. 93,000 acres aflame. And renewal. Yes, life is persistent in the northern forests. After the fire: Wood-boring beetles feed on burnt trees. The hungry black-backed woodpecker follows. Here taps its peripatetic song—the chorus a *you you you—what did you do?*

Ah, praise shrewdness of buried seed. Watch sweet succession of ground plants, of shrubs—raspberry and blueberry. Three years and—abracadabra! Pin cherry and paper birch trees rising—again.

Could we but phoenix ourselves as easily. And patiently await the flowering.

Bawaajige

Whispers through my tributaries—
crane voices and stale pow-wow jokes,
Native tragedy and the "great white road."
I won't cliché you, betray you
with the spent hopes of language.

I am the mirror of your indecision:
Your legs are clan longing
and the echo of honor song beats,
your hands the arithemitized remnant
the treaty-tamed blood formula
of civilized greatness.

Rich man, poor man,
Beggar man, thief.
Somewhere in the fray of the tweeted everyday
Doctor, lawyer
Indian Chief.
we parse and compute identity
in columns of the colonized.
Tinker, tailor—
Halfbreed maker.

Now I am the whisper of a whisper
of old crane voices calling
loud, lusty, and long, the Echomakers
calling across captured ledger marks
like Marion prisoners drawing spirit lines
of imagined motion, riding the regalia of horse nations
overruling simplest computations of victory.

Remember you are the tributaries
the many branchings of tribal nations;
you are the blood passage of belonging.

Do not debate this.

I am not made of bones and teeth.
The fibers of my willow hair
cannot be dissected or carbon dated.
You are not made of Xs and Ys.
Your name is not a formula
or test tube fantasy.
You are the misspelled prescription
written to save the Santa Maria from oblivion.
You might debate this.

The spark of Anishinaabeg stars
the Ponca flame, amber and ancient
ignite the obsidian memory of tribal fires:
The burning wolf eyes of clan brothers
the sweet sage scent of hand drum sisters
the hawk cry of hunters,
the partridge drum and turtle rattle songs
the porcupine quill becoming
of our intricately embroidered lives.
You are the blood passage of belonging.
Do not debate this.

Photosynthesis

Lean in to the absence
the littlest cousin spot empty.
My words come fast—a chant
a dance a sprinkling—before
camera reminds us again
like all crumpled fenders.
But my aunties step in
swing their fleshy hips
toward hope, hands deep
in candied pockets of memory.

Our breadloaf arms baked together
from years of his blue-plaid shirts
beside my lilac scoop neck sweetness.
But today Antell brown eyes
pose, spin another holy cycle.
We add a bundle of hickory thin children
their skin a parchment of piercings.
Our settled feet know: some will survive
some become the hole itself.

Their brown-toed hunger raw
as the scent of funeral flowers
suffocating in the closed-in room.
They arrange and rearrange, a shimmy
and giggle kaleidoscope of t-shirts,
vinyl slogans spilling witticisms—
words stacked like Lincoln logs
a fortress against solemnity.

Exit #135

Call me an aficiando, a devotee,
a Cracker Barrel connoisseur,
yes—a comfort food junkie!
2002, I'm Minnesota bound in a minivan—
two hours from home and its potty-stop time.
Hallelujah. I find a road-trip-mother's salvation.

Hands linked together like paper cutout dolls,
we stumble into this old-fashioned oasis
where the all-knowing corporate overlords
have filled an entire freaking front porch
with honest to goodness wooden rocking chairs.
White rockers, flag rockers, and tot-sized minis
neatly lined up waiting for the wicked and the weary.

Hiding in Madison's freeway corridor—the Heartland.
Here piped-in country music is keeping the beat,
ahh, America, I'm kicking off my shoes and taking a seat.
Thin wood runners flop flop flop across the floor
and the innocent light-up soles of toddlers flash
multi-colored intermittent LED signals for wayside believers.
Soon we've rocked our way to nirvana, the promised land,
or as near as we can get before calling dibs on the bathroom.
Then the inner sanctum summons me like nostalgia or late-night radio,
Dick Biondi's voice riding the airwaves across the sleepy Midwest.
Holy oleo, Batman, it's the American Dream in miniature!
An entire corner of plush pets, talking toys, and giant checkerboards,
a dining room with peg games, dumplings, and all-day breakfast.

I came naïve with unnamed hungers, a tired traveler
in search of a pit stop and old fashioned lemonade.
This voyeurism started innocuously like all retail obsessions
I only wanted a glimpse into the butter-churn, oil-lamp century.
Who knew I would come to crave Beeman's gum and Exit 135—
my visits to these holy relics from another century.

Yes, call me [kon-uh-sur]. Perhaps I am a noun, a part of speech.
My synonyms sound like sugar: savant, specialis, epicure;
or like another calorie-laden Cracker Barrel food: nut.
But I am neither freak nor aesthete, not maven nor cognoscente.
In truth I live as tracker, a sniffer of memories, collector of stimuli—
I am a walking butter churn, a contradiction in terms, or the future perfect tense:
We will have been feasting of the forbidden fruit for years on end.

Speaking, Like Old Desire

Inwe. Mikwendan.
Gezikwendam.
Remember. Or barely. A dialect.
Can a nation re-speak itself
like ghost dance singers conjuring the buffalo?
Who holds the ends of the broken
telegraph lines crackling between
a signal this moment a word.

Like catching a muskie on a crappie hook—
how can you conjugate after forty?
I don't remember, you don't remember. . .
Something bending under the weight of history—
meanwhile, how do you say "snag" in *Ojibwemowin?*
Keep practicing a recitation "My Indian name is. . ."
recollect a drumming in autumn—*Bine,* and the *wiinzowin*
of clan relatives—

Amik Stillday, Anangookwe. Niigaanii.
Make dialect an app and desire a foil-edged laminated prayer card.
These hungry eyes a hazelnut trace,
old power, pictographs red and ancient on rock cliffs.
Yet this crane tongue stumbles again over grammar—
waniike or *boonendan*—what comes before or after
to make forgetting a command?
Will we make spirit houses for buried languages?
Or sing healing songs—*nanaandawi'iwe-nagamonan?*
Speak this future tense in copper like ancient lines, or longing.

Fatima at the Bab el-Bahrain Souk

Brandishing tales of gender-separate wedding parties
and Hollywood-esque female glamour,
you slide your delicate wrist into blue evil-eye bracelets
spread before me the protective *hamsa*.
When obedience is the old wealth, freedom the new,
how to find hands to hold in the fray—
a talisman or safety that cuts both ways?
We finger gold cartouche, amulets, sacred cloth,
even clipped verses from the Quran
deflectors that wake doubt in our own brown eyes:
A protection from every rebellious devil!

Reliquary

Under the midnight aurora
in a northern flannel-sheeted bed,
beneath the weight and wild color
of a yarn-tied crazy quilt,
amid the whispers, tickles, and shushing
of brown-eyed, pony-tailed girl cousins,
I have slept with suicide.

With my bare feet swinging in time
to baking-powder-biscuit stories,
and men spitting watermelon seeds
the shape of my dime-store mood ring,
while truck-driving nomads lift amber bottles
in an everyday larger than Dick and Jane,
I have held danger's bruised moist hand.

On the spinning stools of small town diners
where hopeful adolescents
wear school colors like a cattle brand,
after February basketball chants
where platters of gold or just-cut french fries
pass among friends and Friday night foes,
I have eaten manna with military killers.

In a crowded copper four-door
wearing swimsuit under cut-offs and cover-up,
singing radio oldies along Indiana's highways
on a pilgrimage to any infinity of sand,
driving desires aimless and older than the continent
under the water mirage of the ancient August sun,
I have flirted with the murdered.

Along the simmering sidewalks of Chicago nights
in close jealous crowds that jostle lovers,
weaving between street sleepers and dark-eyed panderers
amid the retractable leashes of urban dogs,
where jazz songs rise against honking traffic
and pencil-thin girls spill like light from doorways,
I have kissed smoke spent from mafia mouths.

Amid the photographic relics of gone bodies
on the darkening veneer of a beside stand,
in a digital world of light emitting diodes,
as age clocks its way toward another transformation
where barely remembered voices count iambic heroic death
and students twitter meaning in 140 characters or less,
I clutch delicate stories—old, never told.

Regarding the Care of Homeless Children*

Seven decades later I trace your *Table X*
easily imagine names of the studied,
Maymie Ellen Bunker, John E. Antell,
Nookomis, Nimishoomis,
those who shelter homeless children—
children of legitimate birth
children born out of wedlock
non-members of family.
With appropriate scientific distance
you count abinoojiinyag—
children with *both parents dead*
children with *one parent dead.*
You wonder why *private homes*
should keep these fledglings?
Depression era White Earth Reservation,
legally adopted
adopted "Indian way"
we call them cousins.

Among the *One Hundred Fifty*
Chippewa Indian Families
on the White Earth Reservation in 1938
you catalogue types of houses—
seventy-one tar-paper shack families,
seventy-one frame-house families,
eight rehabilitation house families.
Your neat columns total incidence—
64 homes sheltering children,
regardless their of type of house, sheltering
78 non-members of family.

Yes, blessed is the fate
of those your *Table X* calls *homeless.*
Chippewa children
brought to live with relatives

taken in as members
by mutual agreement
braided into families
into *tar-paper shacks—*
homes not considered *adequate*
by accepted housing standards.
(Very few of the Indian homes,
you explain, are *considered adequate).*
And owners of substandard
Indian houses do not qualify
for *aid-to-dependent children funds.*

Still those gathered in my bevel-edged photographs
extended families who fished, trapped, hunted and gardened
who followed seasons then years of subsistence *poverty*
regularly took in new members.
Their *inadequate,* drafty, and over-crowded houses
in Lengby and Naytahwaush,
these substandard structures become safe ground
lodges, dens, nests.

And when you summarize findings
regarding the care of homeless children,
Sister Inez your language shrugs
shakes its head, puzzled, as it concedes
the odd futility of this analysis.
The decision to *shelter* these children
grandchildren
nieces
non-family members
to keep them among the community
stitching them in like beads
in a woodland design
holding close the floral hearts of children
was *not. . . related to housing.*

---

* All italicized words are taken from Sister M. Inez Hilger's *Chippewa Families: A Social Study of White Earth Reservation, 1938.*

The Ritual of Wishing Hands

1945 and you stand ship side
a man's body all angles and anger—
myth poking out at your hip,
at the jut of the shoulder.
Yes. A photo. Inherited bones.
How they meander the map of our body,
each dark flap of hair a flag of defiance—
scribbling over the legend, the key.

Each year we drive between water and city
gichigami a harbor—like the memory of you,
like stories carved deeper with each telling—
roads rutted with history of our ancestors
those who traveled through, those left behind.
Hands up for wishes—we've lifted them
years on end like Atlas on the western edge.
But here Gaia in our northern corridor
spills different stories: *anima mundi.*
Soul hold, again and again hold
child's hands in this dark Duluth tunnel.

In the long stretches between daylight
sometimes the shadows crowd between us
dark and broken stories of urban *wiindigoo;*
sometimes we hold our breath too long
like believing and disbelieving is only a game.
In this strange ritual of wishing hands
we flatten fingers against the sky
travel this spine of asphalt—
this dream passage to almost there.

You carried shriveled oranges
in relocation's dark pockets,
carried bruise blue veins and knotted muscles

home to crowded reservation tables.
You spilled the blood coins at taverns
then determinedly unmapped the way
to renamed city waterfronts—
we followed your stories just the same.

Summers on I-35 I believe in a world of betweens:
I am a dock, a wharf, a quay—
a port suspended between shades of blue.
I am a birch, a pine, a notched spine—
leaf green and tawny rooted between earth and sky.
Perhap's Black Elk's red roads and black converge here
where the tired back of Turtle's earth
and the immense sky world of Thunderbirds
meet in the everyday prayers of tiny hands
reaching up to the roof of speeding cars.

Sting Like a Bee

We listened between radio static—back before he was *The Greatest*, before he was Ali. The blow-by-blow coming alive at our kitchen table. My brother and I swung and bobbed between rounds. One pair of boxing gloves between us— we took turns wearing the right. The *tap tap tap* of our padded fists sounded like applause for the real show going on somewhere outside our two-room reservation house.

But we were in it, even then. Wiry brown bodies all looking for a way. Some found Jesus, some fed on the manna of local legends. Golden Gloves boxers rising up.

My mom stepped in the ring every day. We watched her fighting demons she couldn't name. *The hands can't hit what the eyes can see.* Like the *Champ*—dark, tough, and pretty—she had her own phantom punch. Knocked them down quick all through the sixties. We counted—*six, seven, eight*—but never got to ten. Same old hopes same old troubles in for another round. Kept popping back up—like Yogi Bear on our plastic training bag. The weighted bottom heavy as sorrow, as a case of eighty-proof Christian Brothers brandy.

Fight nights though the clamor came from announcers hyped by a left hook. Repeating the same thin laments on style. Hands too low, head pulled straight back. Still no one knew which was faster—his dancing feet or his mouth talking trash. *This is no jive.* So many down in five.

Rez bouts go the distance, but we learned from the come-back king. Take it to the body and hold on. Play the ropes. Three minutes or thirty years, nobody's going to stop this fight and no one goes down easy here. Decades later, back in the center of the ring, still practicing our shuffle. *Float like a butterfly.*

Yeah, it was Cassius Clay all the way.

When We Sing Of Might

i.

In this part I switch clothes with a woman I just met
shed my phone, my metal—pray to the scanner gods.
I walk freely through each lock, each clanging door;
here the prison air, the elastic waist of her patterned skirt
settle like a new identity around my body.

ii.

This is the part where it used to be game—a child
moving like a worm through the blades of cool,
through soft evening grass. Firecrackers our only sin.

From here I watch the patrol car, count to ten to twenty,
count the pointed edges of a star driving by,
remember the chorus about *sin and error pining*—
hold my breath, spend an old longing born of beer,
born of bible talk and men.

iii.

This is the year when no one followed the tin star
or the wonder star of Christmas hymns,
when the trail between the courthouse and my grandma's
grew shorter and everybody's hands got tired
picking the rice clean enough for baby Jesus,
clean enough to sell at the Model Meat Market
on Main Street where all the cars parked on an angle,
and I used to think the sign said "angel parking"
and I wondered who would park an angel
if they could find one.

iv.

Right here *weary world* I park the flashbacks
about all the arrestable moments—a past of illegal
brown bodies eating out of season, boys the wrong color
for love, a past of too many: fish, fists, and bottles

broken, the brown drip of spilled brandy—arrestable
edges of lives made jagged and dangerous
(*His law is love and His gospel is peace*)
star-jagged and dangerous as the moments where I see
and maybe you do too the faces sharpened
into angles of rage, of disgust sharpened
on all the low-wage jobs and lying songs
their children learned in grade school
and sang at concerts with fingerplay
and warm kool-aid, when we all still drank
the kool-aid and believed the liberty lyrics—
(*and in His name all oppression shall cease*).

This is the part where arrestable moments
could go either way—and do
depending upon the time of night
the county and the star-wearing body.
So that quiet grass and breath-holding
was training. That counting, one to ten,
ten to twenty—this is where
seconds can become years for some
when it goes the wrong way
when they are the wrong color
when their pockets are empty
when liberty and justice for all—is all used up.

v.
But when we sing of might, this is the part
the part where my jailed brown uncles
my shackled cousins angel their way in
where children fostered and lost reappear.
I dress in their stories patterned and purple
as night. I dress in old songs of prison trains
and men covering their eyes to sleep,
songs of women on one side of a sliding panel
of lives shattered but mosaiced by might—
the angles of survival a many-cornered wholeness.

The Solace of Forgotten Races

Once more *ogitchidaa* light pipes:
fragrant ink snaking into atmosphere,
a mark upon the solstice sky—ascending
audible as December deer sign.

While today the dow rises falls rises,
truckdrivers sleep to idling engines—
an oasis between eighteen-hour shifts,
and America revs her biofuel frenzy
to conjure from a politician's hat
bypass after DOT bypass, this sleight
of hand, progressive contracted erasure
of rice beds, sheep pastures, clapboard family homes,
and the riverwest Red Owl.

Now in the quiet of the archival moon,
the lost tribes of many nations gather
decipher mythic glyphs hidden
beneath the folded corners of oversized books.
Skillfully we levitate the ochre—ancient
stories meant to be burned painted sung.
Medicinal plants, shields, eclipsed dances,
assembled here in sweetgrass fields of the forgotten.

Outside the bleeping reach of GPS geocache,
beyond the longing of a drive-by economy,
under cover of the intelligentsias' "folk culture"—
a healing drum, the scent of cedar
and origin fires still copper with life.

Again the Night

I wake and listen. And through my open window hear the steady baying
of dogs. Dark minutes I puzzle over their hunt before turning to my own.
Tomorrow in daylight I may find the songs rise from a multitude of frogs
croaking in the flooded wetlands. But at night I arise from my sleep
in a different land. Don't we all.

Sometimes I hear my father's old songs and the clink of glasses as my mother
tidies the kitchen. *Beautiful, beautiful brown eyes, I'll never love blue eyes again.*
She drapes the cotton towel over the metal bar. What sound does that make
in my memory? Reality lies just down the hall—my daughter's muffled
cd-player and the tinkle of wind chimes. Still these never change my midnight
creed. I believe in baying frogs, in the songs of all lost fathers.

Packaged like dreams. The cleft in time. Or parallel lives. Some misty
mornings my mind forgets which world it inhabits. Perhaps I feel a tiny body
heavy across my chest. Baby, dog, stuffed bear? Wait. With eyes closed,
it could be any year.

Yes, believe—we sleep beneath infinity.

Recipe for Remembrance

Western shirt sleeves rolled up, wrist deep in meat, Daddy's mixing. Elbow
out, pop-eye muscles flexed, Eddy's grinding. Big butcher aprons hang to their
knees. The heavy white cotton a palimpsest, mapped with stains. Browning
blood. Pigment of pictograph. Or shroud of time. The cloth speaks of long
Sunday afternoons sung through like these.

Spice tins jig through my father's quick hands—sweet and hardy ginger scents
rise as he tap-tap-taps each measure, thyme next courting mustard seed and
coarse ground pepper, allspice in rich mink sprinkles. Yellowed and crease-
marked, a sheet of school notebook paper stretches across the blue-speckled
counter. In country-school cursive it names each ecstasy in turn: sage, sea
salt, garlic powder, paprika. Now aroma spreads like a fiddle note through the
air. And the hum of old German swells as again his hands cup, lift, and turn.
Fingers dance in cool ground deer meat, pirouette in pork. Speckles of fat flirt,
white somersaulting in red joy.

A bass *buzz* starts up, *sizzles* across the small room. Hot grease *pops* and
splatters as Herman flips sausage patties browned for testing. Crusted edges
cut open, meat steams. A flurry of forks to mouths, bottles to lips. Grainbelt.
Fanta orange. Everybody's tasting, talking, tipping.

Now methodically my mom stretches out casings. Hollow white snakes,
waiting. I take my turn, feed them, slippery and wet, onto the spout that will
spit sausage into empty pig intestines. With ten-year old hands poised, I feel
them fill and slip through my light grasp. Like magic I grow them: auburn
sausage ropes, coils and links, luscious scented rings that will hang in smoke
houses, nubile and expectant. What will they keep of Bass Lake mornings,
grazing, new spring grass, dainty clover? And while their fresh skin dries
and darkens will they too daydream of bounteous breakfasts and the lost
hands who made them?

That Buffalo Hair Fedora

for Rance

i.

Summer dreads on a two-ton buffalo
viewed through the zoom lens of my Canon—
not the sleek and groomed, not the enviable
cooler than trench poet locs
on Quincy Troupe, nor the tough mama
you could lose dimes and pennies in there
hair of rasta soccer coach Michelle.
No, these are the *don't mess with me*
I've got Yellowstone grasslands in my fur dreads,
the *oh yes! you better take your pictures*
from the safety of your van's skylight perch dreads,
and the *I make thunder with my hooves* dreads.

ii.

That buffalo-hair fedora on a long lean Comanche—
prairie strands that withstood snow and wind, gathered
groomed into this dashing caramel-colored topper.
A hat of history sits now upon dark braids. Waist-length,
this hair like bison survival a sublime defiance.

iii.

A colonial greed older than prairie hills
a destiny made manifest in slaughter
of grazing bison, in military-style schools
where our children were herded into classrooms
taught with small tortures to recover
from their primitive and ungodly lifestyles,
where chongos and squash blossom whorls
braids and roached hair dropped heavy to the floor
landed and piled there like gut-shot buffalo.

iv.

That bull fresh from mud wallowing
that massive herbivore has fed on leaves
and twigs, bark, berries, and grasses,
he wears like a crown the evidence of contact
with willow, ash, and especially blackberry.
That wild oxen legendary for head-butting
in rut, legendary too for spring shedding,
will supply soft down we spin and weave,
coarse strands we braid or twist into rope.

v.

Today that sleek buffalo hair fedora, yesterday
tufts of insulation for winter moccasins,
stuffing for dolls and balls,
thread, horse halters, and brushes for paint,
rugs, blankets, girdles, and garters—
yes, buffalo hair sashes, bags,
and earrings, harnesses and hair extensions:
then and now, these buffalo hair dreadlocks
touched, marked by the sweet prairie earth.

vi.

Count then the myriad uses of a hairy clump
the numbers of squandered bison or Native bodies
the things mystical we try to tame
the holy oldness of copper, of order, of name
these micro centimeters between beauty and loss:
that solemn, that survivance—this sweet smooth
this coming from prairie centuries
this buffalo hair fedora.

V.

BLACK ASH
AND RESISTANCE

Unlawful Assembly

Don't hurry to safety.
Each hour your flowered room grows smaller.
Everywhere at the periphery of vision
windows shatter into triangles
of mosaic light.
There in the lonely fragments
a youtube dictator
declares victory,
blood flattens and darkens.
The scent of rebellion
smoke fire and ash
all pungent in the still images
sacrificed to history.
Somewhere the flapping door of an overturned wagon
thumps steadily
in a deserted street—
echoes absent hands.

The Smallest Shaft of Light

> *One can't possess reality, one can possess images—one can't possess the present but one can possess the past.*
>
> *On Photography*, Susan Sontag

i. Zoetrope or the Dream of Motion

Stand here. In this room where heavy curtains block the light. Where closeted chemical scents dense the air. Here eyes awaken in amber. Milliseconds matter. We count exposure. Release stories held tight between sprockets of film. Wait for that magic. Clothespinned moments. The whisper of pages across the length of the darkroom aisles. Small eternity printed and strung to dry. Not Paul Simon's Kodachrome. Not the moving-pictures of train robbery. Not the talkies. But the purity of black and white. Here we shine light through notched negatives. Spill their frozen bodies in unexpected catacomb. Now resurrected. Transformed into image.

This anticipation. This longing. For the moment when the bare white of photo paper darkens into form. The fog of air holding secrets. His closeness in the small space. Was it cowardice not to tell? Timing becomes art here. *My hands rhythmically move the fluid in the tray. The clock ticks. His breath a cadence in my ear.* What can you say into that perilous waiting? *The safe light is on—a quiet hope for transformation. Eyes first then whole faces surface beneath the fluid.* Do they see the moment I become body? *The tongs in my hand. The acrid smell of his arm the chemicals his hands. I lift the photo paper into the stop bath.* Was it illegal in 1978 for a neighbor? *To reach over the arms of a young woman.* Was it misconduct where I grew up? *To slide 42-year-old man's hands against the skin.* Was it betrayal for an employer? *Rough hands inside the lilac slit of my summer shirt.*

ii. Motion and Persistence of Vision

What has disappeared from the field of vision follows beyond. We create illusion. The brain retains what the retina has seen has seen has seen. We lift still sequence into motion.

When movements happen in darkness, how can vision still persist?

iii. Sixteen Frames per Second

Is it also crime if you pushed yourself to safety? If you left the small studio unmarked except for the murky smell sunk into your hair—sunk deep as memory? *How to remember the seconds—my fault, my fault—while feet hit ground around the quarter-mile track.* Is it crime if he dimpled in the dark, his laugh a radio song when he blocked your exit? *How to run like Muybridge's horse, chase shame through the shutters closing on each frame.* Is it crime if he blamed you? Blamed your track-hardened body? *How to spit time back. How to run. Outrun. Spit and tally each circuit—count count each footfall because in numbers it disappears.*

How to remember the disappeared.

I train in darkness. My fingers learn by touch to spool and unspool film. *How to keep my secrets and tell you to unburden yours?*

I carefully choreograph development. Sequence the liquids—a litany ending at fixer. I wash and squeegee. *How the ribcage of my past stands firm. How if he bumps you it is an accident. How my feet unspool new miles.*

In gloom I MacGyver precise cardboard shapes. Steadily shake them beneath the enlarger. My wrist grows tired of these maneuvers—the dodge, the burn. Is it still harassment if he calls you his best friend? Still illegal if he only kept you from leaving long enough to tell you? Only gripped your arm long enough to kiss the moving target of your face, to ruin the beauty of the black and white?

How to find the lush-breasted girl I was in a sequence of stills: Here a drawn copper curtain of hair. Shoulders sunken inward like wilting apple slices. How to unfetal the body. Interrogate that brown-eyed study in deceit. Clothed now in modest postures. Knee-length or longer soothes memory. I know the smallest shaft of light can streak the film. *How to balance survival with truth.*

iv. Kinetoscopes and Peep Shows

Stand here and watch now. See real retreat into history.

The man who was your mentor dies and you never told. He fed you on his own hunger. Visions made with light and mirrors. The muscle and ritual of black and white. If he broke you, you never told. If you changed him, he never told. In darkness where no one else saw.

Ikwe-niimi: Dancing Resistance

365 jingles in rows upon my dress
turned by the hands of one who deserted
escaped a mandated Pipestone education.
266 miles looking backwards for pursuit
hiding from promised punishments by day
migrating like *maang* relatives by moonlight.

365 ribbons hold the jingles to my dress
colorful strips cut tied and threaded
stitched by the laughing women of my childhood,
women who earned 2 dollars and 25 cents
for piece-stitching geese aprons, pot holders
whose stiff fingers tapped drum beats to sew by.

365 prayers swing and tap one against another
zaangwewe-magooday, ancient medicine dress
silver-coned legacy sounding the cleansing voice of rain.
145th White Earth Nation celebration pow-wow
the weight of *anishinaabeg* history on my back
a dress made light by resistance—this healing an art.

This House of Words

You can't take a man's words.
They are his even as the land
is taken away
where another man
builds his house.

   —Linda Hogan, *Left Hand Canyon*

Wisconsin winds carry tribal chants
haunting negro spirituals
songs of freedom marchers—
the syncopated battlefields,
language darkened like wounds.

Low and steady voices drum
words unfurl, wave high like flags
say *the people*
say *liberty, freedom*
say *rights* in every tongue.

Still blue uniforms handcuff songs
in public spaces.
Somewhere in America
leaders still tremble to hear truth
spoken in assembly.

Old people swear
it happened long ago—the theft
of home, our very breath to speak.
The silence they say is old—
old, deep. . . and growing tired.

Mooningwanekaaning-minis

Island home of the golden-breasted flicker, spiritual home of the
Anishinaabeg people. Led by the prophecies, by the sacred shell. From the
east we traveled, stopping where the Migis rose seven times, until it brought
us here—here to an "island shaped like a turtle," to the place "where food
grows on water." This rich land of copper, *mashkiki*, and *manoomin*.

Interlude in fur: courtesy of John Jacob Astor.

Or faith—a priest's palette of heavenly promises, offered to the winter hungry
of earth.

Now read this textbook story of Anthropocene. In imperial hands a magic
act. No scarves or flowers appear, no dove. What flies from colonial barter is
epidemic. See villages flatten before your very eyes. Sign me illusion when
guns become whiskey become paper promises. Abracadaba! Now I see it—the
conjure, the power pen. Lifted like a lance, history a piercing point.

But we recall an older way. Of balance. On Madeline Island, I pound the
golden spike. Symbolize a theft of traditional homelands. There mourn the
Sandy Lake tragedy, the Ojibwe "Trail of Tears." There too claim continuance—
survivance here where the flicker reminds us with its song that we belong. As
long as we remain within the circle, live *mino-bimaadizi*—a good life of respect
and reciprocity.

"Because We Come From Everything"

for Juan Felipe Herrera

Because every earthdiver nation somersaults in origin waters
I claim the holy swimming—dark becoming we share.

Because all the begets and begotten separate by sect
I smudge every line feet dancing each side, erase the divide.

Because we come from everything
from copper earth and the untranslated songs of air
from deep and ancient fires burning now in each traveler's eye
from water's fluid whispers and uncounted beats of silence
the held breath
between border   and freedom
between wave   and shore
between boat   and land
between leaving   and arriving.

Because we come from everywhere
from White Earth and Somalia, from Yemen and Cuba and the Yucatan
our mythic pockets stuffed with blessings for safe passage.
Because alphabet measures of entry and exit
document power
because documents: CDIB Passport Visa DACA Green Card,
block barricade segregate fence enclose—
wall.

Because bans
because directives executive orders
because paper decrees say detain say deport.
Look in the mirror and say *Halt!*
You are under arrest. There must be a law.
because within your bodies illegal blood migrates
because air sneaks through narrow passages
because water seeps into every pore—
build a wall! remove the bad elements, keep nasty out.

Because color-coded dolls and pop-gun mentality teach empire
Because the tweeting talleys of alternative fact infect like plague
Because for some fantasized greatness equals uniform whiteness
Because power, greed, and fascism live on the same block
Because good fences make better metaphors than neighbors
I say wrong to "right-of-way," no eminent domain, no wall.

Because I breathe in your air, you breathe in mine
You give me your breath, I give you mine
Because we share the same elemental dependence
belonging together to this alive place—*aki, nabi, noodin, ishkode*
earth water air fire and the blessed arrival and departure of seasons
the comings and goings of each animal relative
skies hung now with *bineshiinyag*, winged songs of return
no paper trail of identity; only this—
the essential migration of all being.

Because we come from everywhere
We claim this safe earth for all,
in every language—*Anishinaabemowin*, Arabic, Español, Braille, Dakota,
English—we say provide shelter, grant a haven
name me a sanctuary city.

Tribal Mound, Earth Sutra

> *Our wealth abounds*
> *within what we preserve.*
>
> —Allison Hedge Coke, *Blood Run*

We remain
wealthy beyond measure,
the past—ancient treasure we protect.

What power resides in earthen mounds?
Ancestors, wisdom of clan relatives,
astrological continuities, portal to spiritual realities.

Effigy of bird, panther, rabbit, bear
the hungry rise of earth imbued with sacred life,
monument, transcendent force.
Name this site—holy.

Stand with me here
a fragile human thread, earth sutra.
This curved land an ageless link
we a small vibration
one song among the many.

Sing this song now.
My heritage, yours.
Shape in consecrated breath
words that mean: belong
honor, courage, praise, believe. . .
protect.
Transform with me here,
become in this sanctuary
rich in memory,
humble before mystery.

Open the medicine pouch
of your voice,
stand firm together
defend this treasure.
Yes, we remain.

Of the many ways to say: *Please Stand*

i. ∂,Partial Differential Equation
What we erase from polite conversation. Bodies on fire. The historic
cleansing of the landscape, the sweep of humanity west, west, west.
Environmental r ism.

All things being equal, things are never equal. Think of scope. Like the
reach of the imperial. Or consider variables. Value. Or commodity.
Convenience policy, a tally mark across generations. Uranium mining.
Atomic bomb detonation at White Sands. A complicated table of fallout
factors. Plume of greatness.

Shift. Angles and perspectives. Ways of seeing. *Seven generations into the
past; seven generations into the future.*

Or how to solve for survival.

ii. *Zongide'en,* Be Brave.
Another partial differential equation. Let's say a corporation proposes
a mine. Variables include Tyler Forks. Bad. Potato. Rivers. A 22-mile,
22,000-acre strip of land. Jobs. *Maanomin.* Open pit. Exceptional or
outstanding resource waters. Legislation. Iron oxide. Fish. Blasting and
pulverizing. New legislation.

The functions depend upon the continuous variables. Fluid flow, for
example. And changing laws. Somewhere along the granite line, someone
enters. Let's say they have put down one life and taken up another: the
solution of the PDE.

Warriors (walleye, Indian, new-age) face arbitrary functions. Changing
laws. Guards. Guns. If life is stretched over two points. It vibrates. We
cannot measure that vibration in this generation.

We can sing it, or make it into light.

Poem for a Tattered Planet: If the Measure is Life

Born
under the canopy of plenty
      the sweet unfolding
       season's of a planet's youth,
in the trance of capitalism we take our fill
content with the status quo
pull our shades on encroaching collapse
say something about Anthropocene,
the energy barter and the holy fortress of science.

But beyond
the throat of commerce,
beneath the reflection
      of the celestial river,
within the ancient copper beauty of belonging
we stand encircled
      inhabit the Ish,
navigate by the singing of songs.

Though money fog settles around,
confounds measure
today veil of mystery   shifts
lifts for momentary sigh t.
       Here
find rhythm of a tattered planet,
feel on panther mound
a pulse.   Listen—don't count.
Feel small life drum beneath ____.

My core. I am ancient refracted light
or sound
traveling,
my frequency a constant
my voice
bending at angles
to become whole in another surface—
say a poem.

Say a poem
perpendicular to the boundary
of meaning,
make it a prism or possibility
sing of turtle or cast the mythic lumen
of thunderbird   here
on the flat   f alter   of words:

This page   not contract
but covenant.
Sacred where.
Neither image nor voice
will twin itself
In the thick moist   cloud
of being
if the measure is life
each limb   a nimble test   of tree
only glimpse not see   nor calculate.

This Shroud of Commerce shrouds meaning.
In the technology of documentary genocide
in the destructive bonanza of the industrial age—
declare the death of planet
as it passes   through a sound speed gradient
comes out   on the other side
a lost echo of human greed
repeating itself
repeating itself
repea t in g

Each splinter of language
bent   in complicated formulas of inference
of ownership
as fog forgets   then remembers   form.
But we find measure   in metaphor
vibration   earth timbre.
Amid endless metric   errors
of science   or prayer

speak the ninety-nine names for god:
Gizhe-manidoo, Great Spirit, or longing,
Knower of Subtleties,
trembling aspen, the sung bones of salmon,
braided sweetgrass,
the sacred hair bundles of women,
this edible landscape—
aki, nabi, ishkode, noodin,
the ten little winds of our whirled fingertips,
this round dance of the seasons—

the ineffable flourishing.

With mind as holy wind
and voice a frog's bellowous night song
we arrive.
Here sandhill cranes mark sky.
If the measure is life—
their clan legs the length of forever.
Here mirror of lake a canvas of belief.
If the measure is life—
refraction the trigger of all knowing.
Only this.

Now we place *aseema,*
the fragrant tobacco bodies of our relatives.
A sung offering.
To make the tattered whole.
A question of survival.

Of correlation.

                                 Of vision.

The measure is life.

Dispersion: A Treatise

Educating is always a vocation
rooted in hopefulness.
　　　—bell hooks

i.

Where in time
among terrorist cells
relentless fracking
the steady slipping into ocean—
refugees becoming bodies?
Where speak write
or fathom questions
of equity and survival—the dark
lung-hungers of humanity?
In what corridors of becoming
but these?

ii.

Here where inquiry bridges
into the gravitational wisdom
of a collective named science, named art.
Here transform global blueprints,
turn aquaculture lab notes
to sung poetry of repair
to geometry for the flourishing planet.
Where learning bends
to speckled cloth of service:
the simple spooling
and unspooling—of light.

Eloquence of Earth

Nominal signs, these words we use—*future, ecology, seven generations*—
have yellowed into clichés, editorials that line the cages
of captured birds, burn in unransomed stone fireplaces
of America's aspiring, royal mining families.
These green futures cast as fairy story,
sealed beneath the calloused ideals of legislators—
sleek smiling handshakes who seal bargains like Jabez Stone;
Our *I-do-solemnly-swear* paper-promise leaders
enticed by industry frenzy, slight of lips,
the short-sighted tally (seven hundred jobs)
coveted like Stone's seven years of prosperity.
Though publically professed (*against all enemies, foreign and domestic*),
and leather-oath sworn (*will bear true faith and allegiance*),
still *quid pro quos* reign, sell the soul of this land—
our waters our *manoomin* our children, *abiinoojiihnyag.*
Each season gavels strike new bargains with our oldest enemies
maji-manidoog, handsome fast-talking strangers disguised as prosperity.

Daily we watch patient warnings swim the Wolf River,
wash up on the shores of our great lakes,
migrate to absent wetlands, trumpet old calls.
How do we translate the flashing fins of poisoned fish?
What other alphabet do you know to spell *contaminated waters*?
Like banned books words still burn on my tongue—*reciprocity,
sacred, preservation, earth, tradition, knowledge, protect.*
Even the vellum of *justice* disdained, crumbled in quick greedy fists.
Meanwhile we gather here, descendants of *ajijaak* and *maang*
lift our ancient clan voices in longing, for a chant of restoration
in a Faustian world.

If I say *Gichigami*—*Lake Superior*—*a turquoise plain, stretches
infinite, gete-gaming.* If I say *Wiikonigoyaang, she invites us to her feast,*
how many will remember the eloquence of earth itself?
At dawn when *jiibay* mist backstrokes across the copper of northern prairies

eerie white hovering, damp and alive,
will you stretch out your hands in hope
cup the sacred like cedar smoke,
draw it toward you—a gesture
fervent and older than language?
Now I say *wiigwaasikaa*, everywhere we look
there are many white birch,
bark marked with sign, scrolls a history.
I say *ritual, continuum, cycle of belonging*,
I say *daga*, please; *ninandotaan*,
you must listen for it—*aki*.
Yes, our very earth speaks.
Who among us will translate?

Prairie Thunder

Bleached bones. Their empty eye sockets
still seeing the sacred prairie—
this brown fecund earth
round and heaving
like a buffalo's back.

Mashkode-bizhiki—
skulls 180,000 deep,
dem bones rising more than four men tall
to the exact height of colonial indifference.
Bison herds. Their thunder—old
and gone.
Mine on this page—loud
like memory of rifles from trains,
or clatter of 50 million skeletons
bison becoming fertilizer and fine bone china.
This evil, brilliant as the strategy of Kit Carson:
the genocidal slaughter of Navajo sheep—
each the slaughter of a livelihood.

Herd after butchered herd of grassland bison
did not become shield or shelter,
become par fleche bags or travois. Martyred *tatanka*
bodies—not harvested for pemmican or soap
in this insatiable buffalo war. No rawhide
for drums, for stirrups, moccasin soles, or saddles;
no sturdy hair for rope, horns for implements.
No stitches taken with sinew. No arrows
launched from buffalo bow strings—
the majestic skulls of these exterminated
will not grace altars in sacred ceremonies.

See the holy brilliance of prairie light
where placid sun dogs mark ageless skies.
But here bison bodies rotted without tongues
here and here blinding light becomes mirage
where herds appear and disappear on the horizon
like the bonneted Indians in old-time westerns,
or the blue gray of sky transforming to cavalry
where keening winds howl through haunted hills.

Build again the body of a buffalo nation
unstack destruction
toll toll the dance rattle of hoofs.
See the round vowels of these letters
this cursive open like eyes on the smoky dust
of a justice stampede.
Now gather and chant with buffalo calling stone:
see how ridge after ridge fills with brown
triumph, with tribes. This pencil sketch a song
for Standing Rock, a vision of prairie
hills rising rising like resistance. Hear again the thunder
of *tatanka* and *tatanka* and *tatanka*—
the thunder of feet beneath ghost dance shirts
of resilient white buffalo dreams—returning.

Solidarity: A Cento*

i.

Dateline March 17, 2011.

At dawn of Wednesday the 16th, mounted riot police backed by armed forces ~~from Bahrain, Saudi Arabia and the United Arab Emirates~~ attacked, without prior warning, hundreds of families taking part in a sit-in protest ~~at Pearl Square~~ using all kinds of firearms and Apache helicopters and closed all ports to prevent the escape of the protestors and prevent the access of medical aid and ambulances.

Dateline November 20, 2016

On the night of November 20, an army of riot police stand guard as fire hoses blast ~~anti-Dakota Access pipeline~~ activists on a bridge ~~near Standing Rock~~ in the subfreezing cold. A medic describes mass hypothermia and severe hand and head injuries from rubber bullets. People are choking, crying. Helicopters whir overhead.

ii.

Because I was born to this land

> *A woman of earth, I am one in the history of women*
> *Sleepless women for their children's sake*

My people stand for the water

> *I became a woman of water*
> *When from the womb of water, I pushed out my children*
> *As they grow, I tell them about water in the mask of sky*
> *And water latent in the earth*

Because the roots grow out of my feet

> *Water hidden in trees*
> *The water pressed into their bodies*

Because I love this land and I honor the water.

> *I become a women who recites poetry, while lining her laundry*
> *She is aware that each book mentions her name*
> *She knows that she is indispensable.*

My people stand for the water, and they attack us.
How can we stand in the face of violence?

> *I become a woman of fire, when the walls close in*
> *and I am the fuel.*

* Language taken from news stories, the Bahraini Writer's Association website, declarations of Standing Rock activist Ladonna Bravebull Allard, and the work of Bahraini writer Eman Asiri.

Sacred Stone Camp

140 years after Little Big Horn,
after gold hungry prospectors
trespassed onto Lakota land
in violation of the Treaty of Fort Laramie,
new oil hungry corporations
threaten to repeat that history—
repeat the violation of tribal sovereignty
repeat brutality toward Native people
repeat disregard for the valor of earth
the sacredness of the resources of this planet
the waters that give us life.

> When our waters are threatened,
> *I stand with Standing Rock.*
> When tribal treaties are disregarded,
> *I stand with Standing Rock.*
> When sacred sites are desecrated,
> *I stand with Standing Rock.*
> When armed militia mace peaceful protestors,
> *I stand with Standing Rock.*

Moving oil makes money—spilled oil contaminates water.
When 783 million people do not have access to clean water,
when 3,300 ruptures or leaks of crude oil and liquefied natural gas
have occurred on U.S. pipelines in the last six years,
we do not need another precarious pipeline.
The Lakota People will not become rich
from oil passing through their lands—
the Missouri River is their wealth.
In the Dakota plains the people of Standing Rock
do not need the prophesied Black Snake
slithering false promises of energy independence—
the ageless force of prairie winds is power.
If the Dakota Access Pipeline is too dangerous for the populations of Bismarck
it is too dangerous for the Native people of Standing Rock.

When we are not equal under the law,
I stand with Standing Rock.
When the gate price of oil bankrupts our future,
I stand with Standing Rock.
When the fossil fuel agenda bulldozes dissent,
I stand with Standing Rock.
When Indigenous nations come together for Water,
I stand with Standing Rock.

When Indigenous nations gather
to sing, dance, and pray,
we don't need rubber bullets shot point blank
we don't need cavalry history repeated.
At a peaceful protest by Water Protectors
we don't need attack dogs
we don't need faces maced
we don't need women locked in cages.
We need energy justice
we need a leader who says stop
a judicial system that says stop—
stop illegal digging
stop penalizing the poor
stop ignoring climate change
stop fracking
stop desecrating sacred sites
stop endangering our waters.

When Indigenous Nations
from the Sami to the Sarayaku
have sent delegations to Sacred Stone Camp
to stand with Indigenous Water Protectors,
where do you stand?
I stand with Standing Rock.
When Indigenous people are
4 percent of the population,
but stand as protectors

for more than 80 percent
of the world's biodiversity,
where do you stand?
I stand with Standing Rock.

VI.

REFRACTIONS
OF SPIRIT

Minobimaadizi

On the brow of the weakened world
this August sun still spills warmth.
Here where furrowed hands gather herbs,
here in copper memory of *minobimaadizi,*
we camp once more under this canopy of regret,
sprinkle each fragrant offering over fire,
clasp songs tight on throat strings of ancient belonging—
chant belief in any language you know.

> *Aki. Nibi. Gaye Anishinaabeg.*
> *Nanaandawi'iwe-nagamon.*
> Sing healing songs for earth that bleeds,
> the tired waters, and all the tired warring
> peoples. Name the tribes and vibrating cells
> of rock and sweetgrass, of tobacco and sage,
> of shawl, pipe, drum, and rattle,
> of *migizi* wings and sweet cedar-smudge rising.

Here in the strong heart of ceremony
we wait, leaves teaching a spiral calm.
Soon words gather like medicine—
mashkiki, beaded now into seeded images,
into litanies of clan relatives: loon song
and bear stories, the mineral regalia of sky.
Once more echoes of crane calls nourish our journey,
rhythm lifting the sad fever of forgetfulness.

> Everywhere making us whole. *Mino-ayaa.*

A Song for Giving Back

The benediction of Water
begins in the holy *whoosh whoosh
whoosh whoosh* of womb sounds—
this ancient amniotic language
our first song.

Like the earth afloat in a great weeping cosmos,
we fetal beings suspended in sublime liquidity.
Yes, name Water the primary principle, sacred
originating material—
sing our aqueous blood belonging
as what we bless blesses us.
Sing *Spirit of Water.*
Nagamon Zhaagamaa.

Born in the deep wet heart of science
we tell of water—the granite language of earth
the holding and being held
the cabinet of rock bodies seeped through
this spilling.

That the nature of all creatures is moist.
That everything is godfull and growing.
That all who hold with science or spirit
must hold also with change:
liquid to ice, ice to vapor—and back.

The cycle, sung motion,
the water passage of our lives.
Sing *Spirit of Water.*
Nagamon Zhaagamaa.

The benediction of Water
begins also with the *whoosh whoosh* of *manoomin*
the "food that grows on water,"

wild rice kernels falling into canoe bottoms—
into the muddy silt of becoming.

And no arid doctrine of ownership will serve
we river nymphs, minor but blessed beings
we swim if we swim at all in the flood, blood,
wine, baptism, and copper glistening resurrection
of water metaphors for our streaming lives.

Oh sweet sap of trees, oh fertile forest brine
forgive our parched longing and give it voice.
Rivers sing and we with them:
Miigwechiwi—daily make a song offering,
here flows our gratitude

In blue-scented drench of spring
Sing Spirit of Water
Nagamon Zhaagamaa.
In narrow boats on swift flowing passageways
Sing Spirit of Water
Nagamon Zhaagamaa.
When great lakes rush in and tides softly backstroke away
Sing Spirit of Water
As tears stutter from pain, pool and spill
When tongues lengthen, lap and savor
Sing Spirit of Water
When women carry pails and walk for the health of *nibi*
Nagamon Zhaagamaa.
When the body's fluids pulse and yearn
When the liquid vibration of voice rises upward to sky
When seeping in and seeping out meet
When the cup of eternity is full full
Of wet and holy, full full of gratitude
Sing Spirit of Water
Sing Spirit of Water
whoosh whoosh whoosh
Nagamon Zhaagamaa.

When Loving is the Yield

Justice is a blind goddess.
  —Langston Hughes

After harvest
copper rows, plaited and cut, reach
today as ever.
This simplest parallel
straight ahead to the vanishing point,
running like the lines of aging telephone poles
toward many-hued trees, the ache
of rolling fields—of checkerboard
infinity. Of abundance.

Here tiny clusters of farm buildings
lean like a child's cardboard toy.
Haze at the horizon saying
something thin, something gray,
older than distance—
about places where the promise of wheat gold wealth
becomes five barley loaves
and a miracle.

Even now wind drowns this chant
for bodies brown and bent early
in their pursuit of enoughness
for bellies distended with absence.
Wheelbarrows squeak—forgetful
when bounty spills
fall, spools and unspools carelessly
the god we wish for.

Voices in the Desert, Bahrain 2010

Newly sprung from the windswept earth
miles from Manama's sleek seaport of spires and glass,
rising here like a mirage within the ancient world
purpose-built sand-colored walls of change.

> *After birth*
> *the woman is given*
> *a ritual cup*
> *and three dried figs.**

Under this sturdy portico of the feminine
smiling together the veiled and unveiled—
no custom older than education,
none more predictable than the photo.

> *The baby's umbilical cord is buried*
> *in the mosque if it is a boy*
> *in the kitchen if it is a girl.*

Desire as universal as story
as gendered as ritual
The *Royal University for Women*
builds character, social consciousness and community.

> *A rooster or a chicken is slaughtered.*

* Text in right column taken from an exhibit at Bahrain National Museum in
Manama.

Before Pearl Square

Official awards are given, winners feted. Now one hour grows into three and still all eyes follow dark language. My books piled to one side, your poems spread before me like the memory of treaty documents. Translation changes *government* to a word more nearly meaning *victor*.

That I understand, won't change the jobless poor.

That you tell—is another word for *danger*.

Shiteet, the Smallest Pearl

When color and scale of languages
give way to simple b & w of gesture,

When clocks mark prayer five times
each day & chanting voices call,

When your expert hands smooth
wrap & arrange the *hijab* on my head,

Now silently within the Al-Fateh Mosque
belief kneels beside belief.

Canyon on the Edge of Years

An infinity of rims.
My sight adrift pursuing the sand-colored
rust-lined heather-hued peaks.
Ancient. Land that diminishes
the tiny rubble of electronic dailyness.
A tuning of shadows,
of geometric patterns. An ageless dance
as second by copper second
light spills itself, recklessly
now plunges to the tiny sliver of river—
yes, the carving colorado a taper of history.
And we inert and anxious, boot-clad
unweathered in our lotioned, minute humanity.
Hopi call you *Ongtupqa*. Sacred land.
Place of emergence.
Here the dark crags and whorls of becoming,
precipice upon precipice
receding beyond simple sight—
(breath in landscape) this impress of lost gods.
Dream hands that whittle, the pitch of songs
in caves, wing colors on rock walls—
inscribe me here in mountain regalia.

Senbazuru, Held Together by Strings

On my back—like an island sinking

into the familiar pillow of the black and white:

the crenulated edges of your face

photo folded like a paper crane

the origami promise of a single eye

still visible, still seeing me

from the crane's wing, still flying

over my crumbled body—

the thousand cranes

I will never

find.

Spirit Dogs

I'm not much of a walker no more.
Used to be could go all day
with just my gun and my dog
kicking around gopher holes,
checking trap, setting 'em.
Walking dad's woods.

I follow those feet
deep into 1948:
the Antell farm
Beaulieu township
White Earth Reservation.
She walking fast now.
I catch a glimpse
as she bangs out the screen door
hair shining like refracted time
crow-black pixie-cut.
Lunch in one hand,
twenty-two tucked under her arm
she whistles up Larky.
Haven't you dreamed
of that old farm dog
come back to life
her dull matted fur
reincarnated too
lustrous as a loon's back?

Today they wag down the footpath
sniff past lingering scents of skunk
and saw dust that brace the tool shed
in the cabbage-patch reality of memory.
I think she will turn now, see me—pale
apparition from another century—counting

measuring, harvesting, and writing.
I worry my tiresome habits
will stop time or that they won't.
And she does hesitate and turn—
See me, see me. Don't—
but she only waits for the dog's quick tongue
as Larky drinks from the water trough.

Beneath the small dog's green eyes
I know my overgrown gold fish swim
swirling in maddening amber ovals
expanding minute by hungry minute
until they become the metal itself,
their rusty lipped edges spilling secrets
now poured like water onto the packed dirt.
The girl too mouths something
soliloquy I will never hear
 as younger and younger they stand
sunbeam's infinity over their shoulders
on the simple trampled floor of the morning barn yard.

While from behind a white-curtained farmhouse window
familiar eyes watch placid and unworried
of what will befall girl and dog
as they trot on around the barn
then under the pasture fence
and recede into our horizon line.

This is the part I never see;
When she comes out on the other side
is he waiting there with the car
map of North Dakota already tattooed
on the same arm he will raise in anger?
I know she slides in beside him, feels the burn
of summer vinyl on the backs of her legs.
Somewhere a police blotter has notes
about a night intruder, a stolen pig.

Somewhere in a small trailer house
she mails letters, empties ashtrays,
waits with a new dog, Barnick-chinned baby,
and the intricate inlaid cedar boxes
that will whisper to her at night
hold her hostage with their geometry—
block patterns and comforting lies
about change and the prison hands that made them.

Not everyone will wait for her return;
but some draw patience from the soil
gamble on the gestation of winter seeds
hide like old snapping turtles inside their shells.
And look, even the dog has not stirred:
> *I'd tie my lunch bag in a tree*
>   *put Larky there to guard it for me.*
> *Always kept the squirrels away*
> *knew we'd share it when I come back.*
> *Those were my walking days.*

So I set my words like a young girl's dog
just there guarding something
the tree of the garden maybe.
Sun-warmed plums slip so easily
into my waiting hands, my mouth,
or maybe that's another story
other voices telling of the incarnate
ground planted with unknown fruits.
But somewhere, somewhere spirit dogs still sit
and the longer the branches hold their secret
the longer we all walk those woods.

Bronze Lumen

tick of sap dripping,
now flutter-drum of partridge—
palette of spring trees.

copper crane bodies
ride impossible stilt legs
across fields of June

        small fox, backward glance
        tail burnished by autumn sun
        feet first into leaves

hills a smudged sorrel
evening canyon spools light
air holds drum and sage.

        amber-eyed stallion
        mane tangled with winter sky,
        hooves stomp ancient ground.

when snow swirls like breath
vague gusts rise on flat expanse—
ghosts in ocher light.

These Small Turns of Memory

6 a. m.
Syllabus I type
while outside
August lake shivers,
stretches silver
under wisps of fog,
then lifts itself
as from downfilled
sleep.

6:20.
I sip steaming stove-top coffee,
write *Course Description*.
Now sift recollections
of other chill mornings—
in the French village
St. Hippolyte du Fort,
baggy brown pants
sway, the arc of the broom
carrying the sweeper.
I am the swept debris
old streets, detritus,
duty of language.

At 6:32 a.m.
my fingers click on keys,
but on the other side of air
I touch your table.
Again finger the lamp screw,
carefully twist it beyond
black burned edge of wick.
Now the lick of new light
rises behind etched glass chimney,
and shadow companions startle and dart
across sheetrock walls.

Some light still frightens.

6:55 a.m. 6:59
7:08 *Course Requirements.*
In the hyperreal font bank
of my computer screen
I search a color I might know,
some pigment like boiling maple sap
like dried fish blood.
Vital reflection on the eye,
a variant on crayola imagination
like baked dust on a brown beret.

At 7:16 I type *Grading Policies*
and list in mathematical formula
a future.
7:30, *Due Dates.*
Yet
somewhere
half a world away
as I sit in ice-carved stadium seats,
voices of Norwegian children
vibrate the arctic night
they sing the cycle, the sun's return.

7:35. 7:40. 8:00.
LED time accumulates like image.
I let it pass.

And each morning
I still come in slippered feet
steady time at the doorway:
there my blue-sweatered Daddy
old formica table
a small radio before him.
His thick brown fingers curve
like the notes; the beat he taps
bends into some dimension—

not sound exactly
not light,
but the motion of darkness
on walls mime simple
in a world of flame,
some turning of memory
we too trace,
maybe with fingers
folded over keys.

So this is why I write.
Not because my uncle's new horse
tried to roll me off its back that spring,
not because of the Mahnomen sheriff
who, with a body bigger than myth
sunk devil deep into the squad seat
pushing us all to pavement.
I tell you the vote to build
yet another bank, new road,
casino was incidental.

I type *Syllabus.*
8:20 comes and goes.
I add *Reading List.*
Supplementary Bibliography at 8:48.
The province. Not memory exactly.
Not story or language. Nor even pure sound.
Winter count.
The year grandma dodged rabid skunks.
Fuel bills tied in embroidery floss.
Following blue trouser legs
down each thorny path of months,
months not named for roman gods.
Following sun-dappled work boots
to berry patch afternoons,
a dimension both hungry and sweet
red-fingered and flushed.
Don't call it happiness.

Think of the morning lake
the ice stadium the broom
carrying human motion in its arc.
Who can explain the science
of alchemy, the texture of stillness—
one thing suspended
minute in its
turning.

9:22.
Final Exam Date.
Two hours to declare knowledge
in lines and boxes.
I turn from counting and there,
in the sliver space between
one second ticking,
you arrive—a dawn child.
Call it return.
Nothing as accidental as birth order
dictates destiny.
Who knows of sources,
only image and refracted light.
Assembled here like tincture,
medicine color or errand of memory—
as if the alphabet song
were made of scents or gesture.
Each lilt of meaning
like the living flame of old campfires,
like the synapse of a moving bobber
on Pickerel Lake.
Not spelling
but the consequence of the barely visible
filament, line stretched taut between infinities.
How evidence spills from every water surface
that rises and falls as code or sign
fingers gripping the translucent thread—
with life pulling hard on either end.

Winter Aurora

Boots under bath robes
we huddle in the Wisconsin night,
here, too, we whistle
to stalagmite points of light.
Sky shimmers neon
flickers green purple green—
waasanoode
ancient woodland spirits.
The torch of your feet
a northern pathway,
each footfall a spark, a call
to beckon us to the land of *makwa*.
There somewhere in solar wind,
niibaashkaa, dark travelers
lift their muklaks high
dance sky.

After Words

Because the smallness of our being
is our only greatness.

Because one night I was in a room
listening until only one heart beat.

Because in these last years I've
worn and worn and nearly worn out
my black funeral shoes.

Because the gesture of after words
means the same thing no matter
who speaks them.
Because faith belief forever
are only words, no matter.
Because matter disappears
always and eventually.
Because action is not matter
but energy
that spent, changes being.

And if death, too, is a change of being
perhaps action counts.
And if death is a land of unknowing,
perhaps we do well to live with uncertainty.
And if death is a forested land,
it would be good to learn trees.
And if death is a kingdom,
it would be good to practice service.
And if death is a foreign state
we should loosen allegiance to this one.
And if the soul leaves our body
then we must rehearse goodbye.

ENVOI

Drum Song

We begin. Broken geographies.
Silt bodies formed only of longing.

Chart here: Of alchemy inherited
where *Dibaajimowin* spills doppelgangers.

Anishinaabeg water drums circle sound,
spirit echoes refract into honor beats.

Into hungry language angles
of black ash and resistance.

This frayed history we patch
with the patient pitch of story.

Gather now claimed by ancient belonging—
homelands where partridge drum in spring.

ABOUT THE AUTHOR

KIMBERLY BLAESER, an Anishinaabe writer, photographer, and scholar, served as Wisconsin Poet Laureate for 2015-16. She is also the author of the poetry collections *Apprenticed to Justice, Absentee Indians*, and *Trailing You* as well as of the scholarly monograph *Gerald Vizenor: Writing in the Oral Tradition*, and the editor of *Traces in Blood, Bone, and Stone: Contemporary Ojibwe Poetry* and *Stories Migrating Home*. Blaeser is a Professor of English and Indigenous Studies at the University of Wisconsin—Milwaukee, and serves on faculty for the Institute of American Indian Arts MFA program in Santa Fe. Her work has been widely anthologized and selections of her poetry translated into several languages including Spanish, French, Norwegian, Indonesian, and Hungarian. Her photographs, picto-poems, and ekphrastic poetry have been featured in various venues including the exhibits "Ancient Light" and "Visualizing Sovereignty." An enrolled member of the Minnesota Chippewa Tribe, Blaeser grew up on White Earth Reservation. She is an editorial board member for the "American Indian Lives" series of the University of Nebraska Press and for the "Native American Series" of Michigan State University Press. In addition, Blaeser serves as a member of the board of directors for both the Wisconsin Academy of Sciences, Arts, and Letters and the Aldo Leopold Foundation. She lives in the woods and wetlands of Lyons Township, Wisconsin and spends part of each year at a water-access cabin adjacent to the Boundary Waters Canoe Area Wilderness in northeastern Minnesota chasing poems, photos, and river otters—sometimes all at once.